# A HISTORY OF THE
# VAMPIRE
## IN POPULAR CULTURE

This book is dedicated to Gladstone's Library, Hawarden.

My happy place.

# A HISTORY OF THE
# VAMPIRE
## IN POPULAR CULTURE

### LOVE AT FIRST BITE

## VIOLET FENN

PEN & SWORD
**HISTORY**

AN IMPRINT OF PEN & SWORD BOOKS LTD
YORKSHIRE - PHILADELPHIA

First published in Great Britain in 2021 by
**PEN AND SWORD HISTORY**
An imprint of
Pen & Sword Books Ltd
Yorkshire – Philadelphia

ISBN 978 1 52677 662 4

A CIP catalogue record for this book is available from the British Library.

Typeset in Times New Roman 11.5/14 by
SJmagic DESIGN SERVICES, India.
Printed and bound by CPI Group (UK) Ltd, Croydon CR0 4YY

Pen & Sword Books Limited incorporates the imprints of Atlas, Archaeology,
Aviation, Discovery, Family History, Fiction, History, Maritime, Military, Military
Classics, Politics, Select, Transport, True Crime, Air World, Frontline Publishing,
Leo Cooper, Remember When, Seaforth Publishing, The Praetorian Press,
Wharncliffe Local History, Wharncliffe Transport, Wharncliffe True Crime and
White Owl.

*For a complete list of Pen & Sword titles please contact*
PEN & SWORD BOOKS LIMITED
47 Church Street, Barnsley, South Yorkshire, S70 2AS, England
E-mail: enquiries@pen-and-sword.co.uk
Website: www.pen-and-sword.co.uk

Or
PEN AND SWORD BOOKS
1950 Lawrence Rd, Havertown, PA 19083, USA
E-mail: Uspen-and-sword@casematepublishers.com
Website: www.penandswordbooks.com

# Contents

# Acknowledgements

So many people keep both myself and my work going on a daily basis that I don't even know where to start, but I'll do my best. Hugest love and thanks to:

Gill Hoffs (@gillhoffs), who is a brilliant history author, knows how to calm my crazy, and without whom this book simply wouldn't exist; Cressida Downing (thebookanalyst.co.uk) – we must be into the second decade of wailing at each other about writing now? Or maybe it just feels that long; Alex Butler, for endless helpful input and also for kindly allowing me to use some of his own work in the chronology at the back of this book; Tom Bradburn (Friends of Anfield Cemetery) and Brendan Monks (Liverpool City Council), for being so welcoming and helpful in getting me into the less accessible parts of the beautiful Anfield Cemetery; everyone at Highgate Cemetery (that tenth album tho, eh?).

Guinevere Glasfurd (guinevereglasfurd.com), author of *The Year Without Summer*, for her expertise on the weather of 1816; Fran Hansen, for her fabulously vampiric Sims knowledge (and lifelong services to hair); Birgitta Zoutman, one of the loveliest people I know and the absolute queen of cackling at dirty jokes while snapping author portraits; Lucy Chamberlain, font of Discworld knowledge and my go-to fact-checker for the *Rivers of London* series.

Dacre Stoker for being so generous with his time and giving of his thoughts; Wayne Hussey, for tolerating my barely disguised fangirling and for generally being an utter babe; Johnny Brugh, the loveliest vampire I've never met; Kirstin Lavender of Absinthe Promotions who has the best networking skills of anyone I know and kindly introduced me to Dacre, Wayne and Johnny, as well as taking time to answer questions herself.

*Acknowledgements*

Li Zakovics, for keeping me sane on a daily basis (it's an ongoing challenge); my brother, Scott – love you forever; Lee Meadows, who has gone above and (way) beyond for me on many an occasion and who mostly gets rewarded by me being rude to him in return; Jan Hancock; Dr Nadia Van Der Westhuizen, who appears to be constructed entirely of intellect and glamour; Winston Gomez, for Munsters expertise and lessons in Liverpool's more esoteric history; Billy Martin; Lyra Whyte, for her ridiculous levels of Buffy knowledge; Helen Stringer, some of whose thoughts on untangling the psyche of John Mitchell I have used almost verbatim; Jacqueline Dooley Hamilton; Laura Norkett Lui; Steve Kenny; Karen Thomas; Zak Jane Kier, for services to dark erotica; Ruth Douglas; Sam 'Wolf Girl' Cleasby; Susannah 'Tigerlili' Cavill, my fellow blue-furred monster; Mum, Pete and Speedy Nan; the Hoors, who know who they are; Lads – life would be far duller without you; Jim Parkin; Sessha Batto; Johnny Welburn; Jenny Angliss.

Nick Cave, for providing the soundtrack to my life. I'm sorry for my brain falling out of my ears that time we met.

Hugest thanks to Karyn Burnham for her editorial efficiency (and extreme patience in the face of my terrifyingly adept procrastination skills), and also to everyone at Pen & Sword for being so supportive, particularly Claire Hopkins, Emily Robinson and Rosie Crofts.

Dad – I so desperately wish you were here to see that I finally made use of my morbid interests.

And most of all, my boys. Jaime, Oscar – you are the lights of my life and I wouldn't be where I am without you (but if you can stop sending miserable emo music to the family group chat, I'd appreciate it).

If I've missed anyone off, I'm truly sorry – let's meet up in the afterlife and fight it out there. Don't forget your cloak.

# Preface

I can't remember now how or why, but in my early teens I developed a habit of watching reruns of old horror movies. All I knew was that films such as *The Mummy's Hand, The Bride of Frankenstein* and, above all, *Dracula*, had an air of dark deliciousness that I'd never seen before. I felt a kinship with the mythical monsters and Christopher Lee was, to me, the perfect boyfriend. Life in the world of the old horror movies was simple and clear cut – literally black and white, dead or alive. I rapidly became obsessed with this twilight world of death, beauty and barely disguised sexuality. Video tape recorders had not long become available and I would fill tape after tape with overnight recordings, getting up early on a Sunday to watch beautiful women being threatened by caped intruders, before I was forced to rejoin the real world again to spend 'quality time' with my family.

Luckily for me, this was the 1980s and the goth scene was in full flow – a ready source of music, movies and the macabre. I spent my pocket money on cheap Constance Carroll eyeshadows from the local market, wore so much black eyeliner that I looked as though I'd been punched in the face and listened endlessly to *Phantasmagoria* by The Damned, *First And Last And Always* by The Sisters of Mercy and *God's Own Medicine* by The Mission. I sat in the living room of my family's semi-detached house in a particularly boring part of the West Midlands wearing black velvet and matching black lipstick and wondered what I had to do to get a particularly thirsty bat to visit through my suburban bedroom window in the dead of night.

Being human is never easy. No wonder, then, that so many of us see the vampires – forever dark and different – as our one true love.

Violet Fenn
Shrewsbury, February 2020

# Preface

*I was finishing the manuscript for this book when the Covid-19 pandemic hit. As I write this, most of the world is under lockdown and many of us are very, very scared. Hugest thanks to those who continued to help and support me while going through endless stresses and strains of their own – I really hope we're all still around to look back on it all in wonderment by the time this goes to print. Eternal, immortal love to you all.*

# Release the Bats

'But first, on earth as vampire sent,
Thy corse shall from its tomb be rent:
Then ghastly haunt thy native place,
And suck the blood of all thy race'

Excerpt from *The Giaour*, by Lord Byron, pub. 1813

Sleep all day. Party all night. Never grow old. Never die. It's
fun to be a vampire.

*The Lost Boys*, 1987

More than two centuries after John William Polidori wrote *The Vampyre*
and almost 125 years after the publication of Bram Stoker's *Dracula*,
public thirst for vampires shows no sign of abating. Endless books, film
and television shows have portrayed the blood-sucking antiheroes as
everything from seductive lovers to outright monsters – and sometimes
both at the same time. So why *do* modern audiences still hunger for
a pair of sharp fangs in the middle of the night? There are enough
psychological theories to sink the *Demeter*, most of them revolving
around blood, death and sex.

There are plenty of psychoanalytical interpretations of the vampire myth,
most of them to do with lust and fangs and the symbolism of penetrating
delicate flesh. In even the earliest of vampire tales – in the English language,
at least – the themes are heavily symbolic and/or moralistic. Women who
dare to be openly sexual risk being punished by death and men who –
actually, no. It's mostly just women. But we'll come to that later.

*The Giaour*, a fragment of which is quoted at the beginning of this
chapter, was written by Lord George Gordon Byron during 1810–11 while

on his Grand Tour of Europe, the obligatory rite of passage for upper-class young men in the nineteenth century. At its heart it is a tale as old as time – a young woman from a harem falls in love with a non-believer and is murdered by her master for her disloyalty. Her would-be lover – the 'giaour' of the story – kills the master in revenge and then retires to a monastery to pay remorseful penance. Byron wrote in the poem of how the giaour was to be punished for his murderous crime by living for eternity and being forced to feed off his own family by sucking their blood.

*The Giaour* is one of the first known printed references to vampires in the English language and was in itself the inspiration for later 'gothic' literature, including *Tamerlane* by Edgar Allan Poe, a poem of lost love written early in Poe's career, when he was very much in thrall to Byron's literary weight and greatness.

That English-language literary references to vampires are so relatively recent may sound unlikely. Surely vampires have been around since, well, forever?

Perhaps surprisingly, vampires as we know them are a relatively recent invention. 1764 saw the publication of *The Castle of Otranto* by Horace Walpole. Widely accepted to be the first of what would become known as 'gothic' novels, *Otranto* – indeed, subtitled in its second edition *A Gothic Story* – tells the story of Manfred, whose desperate attempts to thwart an apparent curse on his castle turns him both mad and murderous. With mistaken identities, crumbling mediaeval castles, secret passageways and vulnerable maidens galore, *Otranto* is forever the template for the endless glamorously doomed gothic tales that followed.

There were no vampires hiding in Manfred's castle, but there was certainly a monster. Walpole's tale was hugely successful – although it lost some of its popularity when the public discovered that it was a work of fiction and not, as they had been led to believe, the translation of a mediaeval manuscript. Walpole and *Otranto* clearly paved the way for such classics as Mary Shelley's *Frankenstein; or, The Modern Prometheus* (published in 1818).

But it was only with the publication of Polidori's *The Vampyre* in 1819 (itself inspired by a scrap of a story that Byron had written and discarded) that the vampire as we know it sprang into being. The new vamps were powered by blood and lust and invariably had a natty line in tailoring. Thus began our enduring love of the vampire – the bad boys (and girls) of our paranormal fantasies from then on.

Despite being focused around bloodthirsty and mostly heartless killers, vampire stories commonly carry with them a level of eroticism often lacking in other paranormal stories. Even when monstrous teeth are sinking into pale, helpless throats – *especially* then – vampires are sexy.

But why? In this book we'll take a walk down the dark back streets of vampire history, looking at their origins in mythology and literature and their enduring appeal on television and film. We'll meet computer-generated vampires who try to live a wholesome, ethical life and look at the sexuality – and sexism – of vampire lore.

This book is intended as an overview of how vampires are portrayed in popular culture, rather than a chronology or encyclopaedia, and as such jumps back and forth across its subjects with gleeful abandon. I have cherry-picked examples which best illustrate various discussions and for that reason, many worthy examples of vampiric stories and characters are missing, presumed undead. Those mentioned here are mostly my personal favourites – you will no doubt have your own, probably different ones.

'Popular culture' in this instance applies to any illustration of vampiric lore, whether that be historical records, films, television, books or even urban myths. It is unapologetically weighted towards Western interpretations, because that is where the 'classic' vampire began – European legends of the undead were the basis for the vast majority of blood-sucking tales of terror. The undead exist in so very many cultures and histories that it would have been foolish of me to attempt to do them all justice in these pages – there is, for example, a fine tradition of Korean vampire movies which deserve an entire book of their own. I have also included a fair few references and connections to modern gothic culture, as this has itself become almost inexorably intertwined with the vampire aesthetic (and also because I am, at heart, a massive goth).

I often use the word 'vamp' when referring to our undead friends. It should be noted that I am using this as a contraction of the generic 'vampire' and not in the same way that we might refer to a femme fatale, despite the two often getting used interchangeably.

The confusion is, however, understandable, as the word has more than one source. A vamp in its original sense comes from the old French *avant-pied* – 'before the foot' – and is a term used by cobblers that refers to the front piece of a shoe below the ankle. As that part of a shoe was often repaired or replaced, it is also the source of the expression 'to vamp something up', or to 'revamp'. There is a solid argument for the possibility that 'vamp' came into common usage for dangerously attractive women through the overexcitement caused by the occasional glimpse of stocking at a lady's ankle, or the simple act of a woman embellishing her looks.

The more likely explanation is, however, far more prosaic. Theodosia Burr Goodman began her film career in 1914 with Fox Studios' *The Stain*. Realising her potential, Fox set about promoting their new star. A new and snappier moniker was invented. 'Theda' had been a childhood nickname and 'Bara' was allegedly derived from a relative of the Goodman family by the name of Barranger. A suitably gaudy backstory was put in place – Bara was, it was said, the daughter of a French woman and an Arab sheik – and it was noted rather gleefully that her name was an anagram of 'Arab Death'. Quite the radical new image for the daughter of European Jewish immigrants (who actually lived a very comfortable life in Cincinnati, Ohio). Bara's second film for Fox was *A Fool There Was*, released in 1915, which had been adapted from a stage play that was in turn based on Rudyard Kipling's 1897 poem *The Vampire*.

[…]
The fool was stripped to his foolish hide,
(Even as you or I!)
Which she might have seen when she threw him aside–
(But it isn't on record the lady tried)
So some of him lived but the most of him died–
(Even as you or I!)
[…]
From *The Vampire* by Rudyard Kipling, 1897

*A Fool There Was* follows Kipling's original (re)interpretation of the word 'vampire' to mean someone who sucks another dry of what can only be described as their life force. Despite being billed on the film's credits as, literally, 'The Vampire', Bara's character bleeds men of their free will rather than their physical blood. Her erotic powers are such that she compels them to give up everything in favour of servitude to her alone. She seduces men, ruins them, and then, her victim a dried husk and her fun at an end, moves on to the next victim.

Theda Bara is often cited as having been the first real sex symbol of the film industry. *A Fool There Was* was never officially shown in the United Kingdom as it fell foul of the British Board of Film Censors, who held that films must neither illustrate nor promote any kind of illicit sexual relationship. Bara herself found her career curtailed somewhat by the enthusiastic reception her exotic persona received, and struggled to find successful roles that didn't pigeonhole her as the clichéd wanton woman. It is far more likely, then, that our modern interpretation of 'vamp' springs from Bara's engaging turn as a femme fatale.

In my world, however, vamps are vamps, regardless of their sex, creed or colour. Some really great examples have been omitted in favour of some pretty awful ones, because it wouldn't be very interesting if I just wrote a list of enjoyable movies and books.

This isn't a vampire encyclopaedia, nor is it an exhaustive critical guide. What I have tried to do instead is take readers on an enthusiastic romp through the ways we have viewed and perceived vampires over the centuries, with a closer focus on their increased presence in popular media across the last 200 years or so. When it comes to films, books and music that I like, I am a complete fangirl and make no apologies for that. Some of the people I've spoken to for this book have even seemed a bit confused as to why I would be so interested in either them or their work – the simple answer is that I am fascinated by people who think, write and create differently. This applies to everyone and everything I've included in these pages, from the writers of nineteenth-century classics to the person in the present day who creates imaginary people on her computer and puts endless hours of time and effort into making her vampires just that little bit different.

Vampires have always existed in our heads, even before we gave them a name. They might prefer to stay in the shadows, but there is a huge amount of fun to be had in watching – at a safe distance – and learning from them. When it comes to our innermost and most secret desires, blood and lust are often more closely entwined than we realise.

The vampire is within all of us.

# Chapter One

# On the Origin of Vampires

For the life of the flesh is in the blood – Leviticus, 17:11

Prior to the nineteenth century, vampires didn't exist – or at least, not in the form we would recognise today. Before the advent of gothic literature, those creatures we would describe as 'vampires' were not only universally feared and loathed, they were often also physically ugly. The etymology of the word 'vampire' is itself uncertain, but is widely assumed to have come from the Hungarian *vampir*, itself rooted in the Old Church Slavonik *opiri*. The name certainly appears to be Slavic in origin, so it comes as no surprise that the vast majority of 'old' vampire stories originate in Eastern Europe.

Different cultures have had varying ideas of what constitutes a 'life-sucking' creature over the centuries. Ancient Greek mythology tells of Zeus's wife Hera discovering his infidelity with Lamia and killing all of Lamia's children (or possibly compelling Lamia to kill them herself); she compounded Lamia's agony by inflicting her with insomnia. In order that she might get some peace, Zeus – ever the caring boyfriend – gave Lamia the ability to remove her eyes. The erstwhile mistress got her twisted revenge on humanity by sucking the blood of young children while they slept. Over the centuries, the concept of a 'Lamia' shifted and in many tales became a deadly seductress who enticed and devoured young men, to all intents and purposes a succubus – a female demon who seduces men in their sleep.

A Jewish story from *Sefer Hasidim* – the *Book of the Pious*, written around the turn of the thirteenth century – talks of Astryiah, an elderly female vampire who sucks victims' blood through her hair (rather unhelpfully, there is no further detail as to how this might work). The assumption is that Astryiah was an 'estrie', a creature that can fly and assume different forms in order to catch and suck the blood of their victims. And should you ever be unfortunate enough to fall victim to the bite of an estrie, the (rather unusual) antidote is to eat her bread and salt.

Interestingly, the same collection of writings include a method for killing witches which sounds rather similar to that believed to have been used against vampires:

> Know too that there was a witch, an estrie, who once was caught by a man. He said to her, Do not [try to] escape from my grasp, as you have caused numerous deaths in the world. What can I do to you so that after your death you will not consume [people's flesh]?
>
> She said to him, If you find [an estrie] in the grave with her mouth open, there is no remedy, for her spirit will attack the living. And there is no remedy unless a spike is hammered into her mouth and into the earth. Then she will attack no more. And for this reason, one should fill her mouth with stones.
>
> From the *Sefer Hasidim*, trans. Rabbi Eli D. Clark, 2011

The *impundulu* of Africa's eastern Cape was a vampire who took the role of a witch's familiar. Usually appearing as the large black and white 'lightning bird' (possibly based on the hamerkop wading bird, which is native to the area), the witch had to be careful to keep her impundulu well fed, or risk it turning on her. Most often believed to be a small bird that lived off human blood, it is sometimes portrayed as a beautiful young man. An impundulu would be passed down from the witch to her daughter (assuming he hadn't eaten her first).

It is noticeable that many of the oldest 'vampire' stories tell of women killing babies and children. It's possible that this may have arisen from cases of what we would today call 'sudden infant death syndrome' (SIDS), or 'cot death'. Infant mortality was very high in most cultures up until relatively recently and the further back we go into history, the less background knowledge people had of the reasons for their unexpected and tragic losses. There was also less awareness of what constituted a healthy diet – and certainly less scope for providing it, even if dietary requirements were understood – with infants put at risk of becoming malnourished without anyone even realising what was happening.

A child could quite easily be put to bed at night seemingly hale and hearty, only for its parents to discover it lifeless the next day. In those times when religion played more of a part in the education of the populace than science, bereaved parents would all too often conclude that it had been caused by something not of this world.

Remember, also, that throughout history the majority of babies have been breastfed, whether by its own mother or a wet nurse. If anything then happened to the child, the blame was likely to be laid on the woman who had care of it at the time. That said, mortality rates were often such that losing a child was, during some periods of history, considered par for the course. Given that contraception and other family planning was all but non-existent, dead babies were, at times, merely collateral damage – the 'lost ones' dotted among their siblings who survived.

The 1800s were a more credulous and curious time. This was an era during which Arthur Conan Doyle genuinely believed there were fairies at the bottom of the garden and spiritualism led even the most pragmatic members of society to take part in seances in the hope that it would bring them closer to God. Society was moving and adapting at high speed, the second Industrial Revolution bringing with it changes in technology that on occasions must have appeared to be, quite literally, magical. Across the globe society was changing, for better or worse. Many found themselves turning to different forms of spirituality in order to keep some form of stability, or clung to old beliefs as a safety net as everything changed around them. Author Gill Hoffs describes the delicately balanced dichotomy of the Victorian intellect in her book, *The Sinking of RMS Tayleur*:

> Victorian Britain was a strange cultural mix of glory and guilt, prim delicacy and delight in the macabre. The world was changing at a frightening rate [...] a time of industrial development and discovery, yet [...] newspapers reported incidents of witchcraft as fact.

Over the course of the nineteenth century, what's sometimes referred to as the 'vampire panic' took hold in New England in the United States. Tuberculosis was running riot across the region and in the absence of medical understanding it was often believed that the disease was being spread by the dead returning to steal the life force of their surviving relatives. Widely known as 'consumption' for the way it appeared to consume its victim's health, TB was, and is, highly contagious, spreading rapidly through households in an era of lower hygiene standards. It's perhaps not surprising that theories developed which suggested that the first victim of the disease drained the life force of others in the house as they struggled to survive.

Lena 'Mercy' Brown was the 19-year-old daughter of George and Mary Brown, who lived in the town of Exeter, Rhode Island. Mary died of tuberculosis in 1883, followed by eldest daughter Mary Olive in 1886. Mercy and Edwin, George's remaining children, contracted the disease in 1891, with Mercy dying in January 1892. By this time, friends and neighbours were beginning to suspect foul play of the supernatural kind. They persuaded a rather reluctant George to disinter his loved ones' bodies in order to check for undead goings-on, in the hope of saving the still-ailing Edwin.

The bodies of both Mary and Mary Olive were discovered to be at stages of decomposition consistent with the length of time they had been buried, but Mercy's corpse appeared to be 'fresh', apparently showing no sign of decomposition. A local doctor raised objections, pointing out that Mercy had been dead for less than two months during the coldest time of year (her coffin had in fact been kept in a crypt for some time, as the frozen ground was too hard to dig a grave), and a lack of decay was therefore to be expected. He even removed the dead girl's lungs, insisting that they showed signs of tuberculosis (the disease, already acknowledged for centuries, had been formally recognised by the medical profession since the early 1800s). It was to no avail. His protests were ignored in favour of superstition and Mercy's heart and lungs were cut out in order to be burned on a pyre constructed on nearby rocks.

In the hope of saving Edwin's life, the ashes of his sister's vital organs were mixed with water and given to him as a medicinal concoction. Unsurprisingly, this rather unpleasant 'cure' failed utterly, and despite the extreme efforts, Edwin died on 2 May, 1892.

In the days before scientific knowledge of diseases such as tuberculosis, a spate of deaths for apparently no reason would have been terrifying for most people. There was no way of knowing who would be next, or why some people died and not others. Humans have, for almost all their existence, taken refuge in folk tales. Winding fear into superstition gives us a semblance of control, no matter how elusive that control might actually be. There is little more terrifying than impotence in the face of disaster – better to create a target upon which to vent one's anger and to use as a focus for the un-channelled fear.

Fear of the undead has led to mass accusations in the past. In the early 1700s there was a spate of apparent sightings in eastern Europe, resulting in the hunting and staking of supposed vampires. In what is sometimes known as 'the eighteenth-century vampire craze', entire villages became convinced they were being invaded by vamps, digging up suspect corpses in order to stake them.

In 1731, thirteen deaths occurred in one Serbian village in close enough succession to unnerve the local population, and a doctor specialising in infectious diseases was sent to the village to find out what was going on. His verdict that the deaths were almost certainly due to malnutrition was too simple an explanation for the residents, who insisted that the deaths were in fact due to attacks by vampires. The doctor was persuaded to exhume the suspect corpses. Much to his surprise he discovered that not only did the bodies not appear to have decomposed, their mouths appeared to contain what he believed to be fresh blood.

Disbelieving officials in Vienna sent respected military surgeon Johann Flückinger to check on the doctor's findings, along with other doctors and army officers as witnesses. Not only did Flückinger and his companions find no major decomposition on many of the bodies, they also agreed that if anything, the bodies had taken on a 'plump' appearance.

Thanks to Flückinger's report, the Serbian vampire epidemic was the first to be fully documented. He goes into extensive detail for many of the victims and has clearly accepted that vampirism can be the only logical explanation for such strangeness.

> A woman by the name of Stana, 20 years old, who had died in childbirth two months ago, after a three-day illness, and who had herself said, before her death, that she had painted herself with the blood of a vampire, wherefore both she and her child – which had died right after birth and because of a careless burial had been half eaten by the dogs- must also become vampires. She was quite complete and undecayed. After the opening of the body there was found in the cavitate pectoris a quantity of fresh extravascular blood. The vessels of the arteries and veins, like the ventriculis ortis, were not, as

is usual, filled with coagulated blood, and the whole viscera, that is, the lung, liver, stomach, spleen, and intestines were quite fresh as they would be in a healthy person.

[...]The skin on her hands and feet, along with the old nails, fell away on their own, but on the other hand completely new nails were evident, along with a fresh and vivid skin. [...] There was an eight-day-old child which had lain in the grave for ninety days and was similarly in a condition of vampirism.

From the report of Johan Flückinger, 1732

Not wanting to risk a reoccurrence of the incident, Flückinger and his men cut the heads off the vampire corpses before reburying them.

This was not the first incident of deadly vampiric outbreaks in the area. In 1726, a Serbian *hadjuk* (which roughly translates as a member of an irregular peasant infantry) by the name of Arnold Paole died after falling from a hay wagon and breaking his neck in the village of Trstenik, on the banks of the West Moravia River in central Serbia.

Prior to his death, Paole had complained of being 'plagued' by a vampire some years before, probably in the area we would now know as Kosovo. He had only escaped, he claimed, by eating soil from the vampire's grave and covering himself with blood (one can only wonder quite how smearing oneself with blood could protect against blood-drinking vampires). So when villagers began to fall ill not long after Paole's death, the conclusion was simple. The Kosovo vampire must have infected Paole – and the hadjuk was now taking his turn as a murderous creature of the night.

Paole's body was disinterred, the horrified villagers discovering that his corpse showed no signs of decomposition. Indeed it was claimed that, similarly to examples in Flückinger's report, the nails on his hands and feet had fallen off and been replaced by freshly grown replacements. Not only that – it was said that when Paole's body was staked, he shrieked and bled from the entry wound. Clearly feeling that it was better to be safe than sorry, Paole's erstwhile neighbours decided to take the safest option and cremated his remains.

Such stories were gruesomely fascinating enough to be taken up by the press of the time, with even London newspapers reporting on how, in dim and distant European lands, the undead would rise from the grave and suck the blood of the living. The idea of the vampire took hold enough that in the mid-eighteenth century, the Earl of Sandwich named one of his racehorses 'Vampire', clearly already recognising its potential as a glamorous and powerful description, as well as an intimidating one.

Another tale from Serbia made the news in the latter part of the nineteenth century. On 24 July 1870, a story appeared on page four of the *Daily Alta California* newspaper in San Francisco, titled rather alarmingly,

> VAMPIRES: Gibbering Ghosts in Germany—A Flesh-Creeping Narrative of Vampirism—Truth Stranger Than Fiction

It was an almost direct reprinting of an article from *The New York World*, whose reporter had, apparently, suffered a terrifying experience while travelling in Hungary. Waking in the early hours in a panicking cold sweat, the reporter found himself pinned to the bed by 'some horrible thing, cold as death, that lay upon my breast, pinioning my arms to my sides and trying to fasten its clammy mouth upon my throat.' Having been disturbed by others alerted by the man's screams, the monster of the night escaped through a window. The *World*'s reporter was, he tells us, inspected by his landlord for signs of a vampire attack and was most relieved to discover that 'there was no trace of puncture there'.

Being a responsible journalist, our man from the *World* decided to investigate the landlord's claims that this was far from being the first attack of its kind. In fact, only the previous night three villagers had died having had 'their blood sucked from their bodies' by no less than the Devil himself.

Heading to the local churchyard, the reporter found a group of local men preparing to open the grave of one Peter Dickowitz. Dickowitz had, his erstwhile neighbours claimed, been harassing residents of the village – despite having died three weeks previously. Having claimed in life to have survived a vampire attack in his youth, Dickowitz had clearly, according to the villagers, finally succumbed to the inevitable. The only way to stop the murderous rampage of the resident vampire and his victims, they insisted, was to disinter any suspect corpses and stake them through the heart.

The newspaperman didn't hold back any details in his lurid report. As three coffins were opened, he apparently leaned forward to get a closer look, noting that, 'the men within them were not dead; but horrible beyond expression, deadly in their ghastliness, yet alive, they lay there. Their bodies were swimming in blood, and a horrible leer was on their mouths, and anguished fate within their staring eyes.'

Not one for descriptive subtlety, our man continues, 'Loathsome beyond thought, deadly beyond nightmare dream, they were the living dead.' He goes on to describe how the corpses were pulled from their coffins and staked, whereupon, 'there came from each such a wailing sob and cry as never did I dream even in nightmare.' Having witnessed the terrible creatures meeting their even more terrible end, our hero sighed wearily and headed for home.

The trouble with this otherwise detailed and well-referenced account is that it is almost certain that none of it actually happened. The story shares too many close details with that of Arnold Paole back in the early 1700s, including the very specific way that Dickowitz apparently 'cured' himself of vampirism while still alive by eating soil from his attacker's grave and covering himself with blood.

Even as far back as 1870, newspapers knew that nothing attracts an eagerly voyeuristic audience more than a dramatic tale from foreign climes. If their man on the spot could be witness to behaviour that would never be allowed happen on the more civilised shores of the western world – and better still, could be deeply involved in it before turning his back on such animalistic behaviour in a suitably superior manner, readers would lap it up. Peter Dickowitz was, in all likelihood, nothing more than the nineteenth-century version of clickbait.

There are many tales of disinterred corpses having blood around their mouths, or even in their stomachs. One has to bear in mind that most of these tales pre-date modern medical knowledge of what happens to bodies after we die.

Purge fluid is the result of the breakdown of various body tissues in the corpse as decomposition begins to take hold. As pressure builds up inside the body, the decaying liquid is forced out. It seeps from all orifices, but the ones where it is most commonly seen – for fairly obvious reasons – are the mouth and nose. Although it may appear to be red-black and therefore easy to mistake for blood, purge fluid is actually the caused by the decomposition of the gastrointestinal tract. The fluid also builds up in the main body cavities, which would certainly give the impression of 'bleeding out' should one stake such a body and give the fluid an exit route. One also has to wonder whether perhaps the story of Paole's corpse 'shrieking' when it was staked might not be based on some level of truthfulness. It isn't beyond the realms of possibility that the noise might have come from gasses building up inside the corpse, which were perhaps released under pressure when it was staked.

What is certain is that suggestibility played a huge part in these events. Anecdotal evidence points to many disinterred corpses actually being in the expected state of decomposition for the length of time since death, but people often see what they want to see. If you have been wound up to the point of hysteria about a 'vampire threat' and are taking part in a mass hunt for the culprits, you are unlikely to step back and say 'well actually, that one looks pretty dead to me', especially if your companions are merrily chopping off heads and banging stakes through mouldering bodies. Humans are suggestible creatures and instinctively show herd behaviour when faced with a threat. There is also always an inherent risk in going against a crowd who might turn on anyone who disagrees with them. We see this happen to this very day, with mob-mentality and vigilante attacks – when questioned after the event, it's inevitable that some of the people involved will confess to having simply been carried away by the excitement and adrenalin of the hunt.

Rather than dismembering or disinterring corpses, some vampire hunters would push a large stone into the decaying jaw of a suspected vampire, wedging it firmly between the teeth so that the mouth wouldn't move. This, it was believed, would prevent the vampire from feeding, and thus it would starve to its final death.

Walter Map, an associate of Thomas Becket, was a mediaeval writer who specialised in retelling folk stories and historical anecdotes. In effect, Map was an early gossip columnist, collecting and curating stories of mostly unprovable veracity. In *De Nugis Curialium*, (usually translated as 'Courtier's Trifles'), written in the twelfth century, Map recounts tales of what we today would call vampires, although at that time they were more generally referred to as 'revenants' – simply, 'the undead'.

The then Bishop of Hereford, Gilbert Foliot, was once apparently asked to give advice on how to kill a vampire. Having been begged by an English knight, William Laudun, for advice on dealing with a 'Welshman of evil life' who refused to stay dead, preferring to rise nightly from his grave in order to curse his erstwhile fellow villagers, Foliot declared:

> the Lord has given power to the evil angel of that lost soul to move about in the dead corpse. However, let the body be exhumed, cut the neck through with a spade, and sprinkle the body and the grave well with holy water, and replace it.

From *De Nugis Curialium*, trans. M.R. James

Map clearly lived in a time when the clergy were busy with strange requests of all kinds. He tells of how Roger, Bishop of Worcester, ordered a cross to be laid on the grave of a man who, despite having been firmly buried after an 'unchristian' death, insisted on wandering about in his shroud for more than a month, terrifying the local populace. The cross trick apparently worked – the deceased sank into the soil and finally remained there, having clearly learned his lesson.

Map wasn't alone in his chronicling of the mediaeval undead. Around the same time, William of Newburgh wrote *Historia Rerum Anglicarum*, or *History of the Affairs of the English*, in which he touches on the idea of revenants rising from the grave. Newburgh claimed to be unbiased by personal beliefs and recounted tales of supernatural happenings with no claim as to their veracity, but – as was common for the time – clearly believed in the potential possibility of life after death.

Antoine Augustin Calmet was a Benedictine monk who lived in what is now the Lorraine region of France. Born in 1672, he was a renowned academic who was admired by many. The French philosopher Voltaire is believed to have visited Calmet at his abbey in Senones on more than one occasion (and Voltaire has quite the opinion on vampires himself, as we shall see). Calmet was exceptionally well-read for the time and wrote many books of his own, including a treatise on the mysteries of the occult. First published in 1746 and then revised and extended in 1751, '*Dissertations sur les apparitions des anges, des démons et des esprits, et sur les revenants et vampires de Hongrie, de Bohême, de Moravie et de Silésie*' is also known by the rather less convoluted translation, '*The Phantom World: the History and Philosophy of Spirits, Apparitions, &c.*'

In it he quotes from *Lettres Juives* ('Jewish Letters') – an epistolary novel that had been published in 1738 and which is widely attributed to French author and religious critic, Jean-Baptiste de Boyer, Marquis d'Argens.

We have just had in this part of Hungary a scene of vampirism, which is duly attested by two officers of the tribunal of Belgrade, who went down to the places specified; and by an officer of the emperor's troops at Graditz, who was an ocular witness of the proceedings.

In the beginning of September there died in the village of Kivsiloa, three leagues from Graditz, an old man who was sixty-two years of age. Three days after he had been buried, he appeared in the night to his son, and asked him for something to eat; the son having given him something, he ate and disappeared. The next day the son recounted to his neighbours what had happened. That night the father did not appear; but the following night he showed himself, and asked for something to eat. They know not whether the son gave him anything or not; but the next day he was found dead in his bed. On the same day, five or six persons fell suddenly ill in the village, and died one after the other in a few days.

The officer or bailiff of the place, when informed of what had happened, sent an account of it to the tribunal of Belgrade, which dispatched to the village two of these officers and an executioner to examine into this affair. The imperial officer from whom we have this account repaired thither from Graditz, to be witness of a circumstance which he had so often heard spoken of.

They opened the graves of those who had been dead six weeks. When they came to that of the old man, they found him with his eyes open, having a fine colour, with natural respiration, nevertheless motionless as the dead; whence they concluded that he was most evidently a vampire. The executioner drove a stake into his heart; they then raised a pile and reduced the corpse to ashes. No mark of vampirism was found either on the corpse of the son or on the others.

Thanks be to God, we are by no means credulous. We avow that all the light which physics can throw on this fact discovers none of the causes of it. Nevertheless, we cannot refuse to believe that to be true which is juridically attested, and by persons of probity.

Although *Lettres Juives* is now believed to be a work of fiction, Calmet was not the only one who believed it to have been written as fact. He was, however, perhaps the most critical of all its many readers. In a chapter titled 'Arguments Of The Author Of The "Lettres Juives", On The Subject Of These Pretended Ghosts', Calmet declares his disbelief quite forcibly.

> There are two different ways of effacing the opinion concerning these pretended ghosts, and showing the impossibility of the effects which are made to be produced by corpses entirely deprived of sensation. The first is, to explain by physical causes all the prodigies of vampirism; the second is, to deny totally the truth of these stories; and the latter means, without doubt, is the surest and the wisest.
>
> But as there are persons to whom the authority of a certificate given by people in a certain place appears a plain demonstration of the reality of the most absurd story, before I show how little they ought to rely on the formalities of the law in matters which relate solely to philosophy, I will for a moment suppose that several persons do really die of the disease which they term vampirism.
>
> I lay down at first this principle, that it may be that there are corpses which, although interred some days, shed fluid blood through the conduits of their body. I add, moreover, that it is very easy for certain people to fancy themselves sucked by vampires, and that the fear caused by that fancy should make a revolution in their frame sufficiently violent to deprive them of life.
>
> Being occupied all day with the terror inspired by these pretended ghosts or revenans, is it very extraordinary, that during their sleep the idea of these phantoms should present itself to their imagination and cause them such violent terror? that some of them die of it instantaneously, and others a short time afterwards? How many instances have

we not seen of people who expired with fright in a moment? and has not joy itself sometimes produced an equally fatal effect?

Considering the religious and spiritual era in which he lived, and given that he was a 'man of God' himself, it is interesting to see just how scientifically Calmet dissects what he clearly believes to be instances of some form of hysteria. He suggests that beliefs in revenants, vampires and the undead in general may have developed from old burial customs. The bereaved were in the habit leaving symbolic offerings on the graves of the deceased and the offerings – usually of food and wine – were then left in place for the poor. Calmet's logic seems to have been that it isn't much of a leap for a credulous society to translate symbolism into reality, rapidly developing a belief that the dead really were 'coming back to life' in order to consume the gifts that had been left.

> Now, if they believed that the dead ate in their tombs, that they could return to earth, visit, console, instruct, or disturb the living, and predict to them their approaching death, the return of vampires is neither impossible nor incredible in the opinion of these ancients.

Calmet's own beliefs stay firmly on the side of the sceptical.

> But as all that is said of dead men who eat in their graves and out of their graves is chimerical and beyond all likelihood, and the thing is even impossible and incredible, whatever may be the number and quality of those who have believed it, or appeared to believe it, I shall always say that the return (to earth) of the vampires is unmaintainable and impracticable.

Voltaire, writing in his *Dictionnaire philosophique* of 1764, had his own interesting take on the vampire myth – one that might have raised an eyebrow of his old friend Calmet.

> [...] the true vampires are the monks, who eat at the expense of both kings and people. [...] We never heard a word of

vampires in London, nor even at Paris. I confess that in both these cities there were stock-jobbers, brokers, and men of business, who sucked the blood of the people in broad daylight; but they were not dead, though corrupted. These true suckers lived not in cemeteries, but in very agreeable palaces.

His words were echoed by Karl Marx, who in 1867 declared: 'Capital is dead labour, that, vampire-like, only lives by sucking living labour, and lives the more, the more labour it sucks.'

The definition of vampirism has never been a clear one. It is the relatively modern world that has honed the definition to that which we know so well today.

Taphophobia is the fear of being buried alive (its antonym being 'taphophilia' – a fascination with funerals, graveyards and death culture in general). In the centuries before science and medicine had worked out just what, precisely, constituted 'dead', this wasn't an irrational fear to have. There is reasonable cause to believe that at least some of Map's tales and others like them – of ordinary folk rising from the grave to terrify the loved ones they'd left behind – may have been true, at least in part. Some cases could, perhaps, be explained by the horrors of premature burial. In times before there was any real scientific knowledge of how the human body worked, people were occasionally presumed dead, when in reality they were merely deeply unconscious. On Thursday 6 December 1877, the *Dundee Courier* reported on a bloodcurdling case from Naples:

> some time ago a woman was interred with all the usual formalities, it being believed that she was dead, while she was only in a trance. Some days afterwards, the grave in which she had been placed being opened for the reception of another body, it was found that the clothes which covered the unfortunate woman ware torn to pieces, and that she had broken her limbs in attempting to extricate herself from her living tomb.

The newspaper goes on to report that both the doctor who had signed the 'certificate of disease', and the mayor who had given permission for interment were each sentenced to three months imprisonment on the charge of involuntary manslaughter. But verifiable cases of premature burial are thin on the ground – and it is unlikely that it has ever been overly common, even in less scientific times. This doesn't stop it being a terrifying prospect, of course.

Edgar Allan Poe used taphophobia in several of his stories, including the rather literally titled *The Premature Burial*. In it, Poe tells the story of a man who suffers from cataplexy – a condition in which one falls into a trance and is unable to move, but remains fully conscious. He becomes increasingly wretched with the fear of being buried while in one of these episodes, until he wakes up in what he believes to be a coffin. His tomb actually turns out to be a ship's cabin bed and the shock is enough to cure him instantly of his phobia.

Renowned for his over-anxious behaviour – he was terrified of both dogs and fire, among many other things – Danish author Hans Christian Anderson also had a longstanding fear of being buried alive. He regularly left a notecard on the bureau next to his bed which read, 'I only appear to be dead' (one wonders whether Terry Pratchett was inspired by this while writing his *Discworld* novels, given Granny Weatherwax's habit of leaving a sign saying 'I ATEN'T DEAD' balanced on her bony and apparently deceased chest when she went out mentally travelling of an evening). Anderson spent his last few days with long-time friends Moritz and Dorothea Melchior at their home in Copenhagen. Realising that the end was near didn't ease Anderson's concerns one bit – he asked Dorothea to promise that she would cut his veins after he died, just to be on the safe side.

What is certain is that if a 'corpse' regained consciousness after burial, it wouldn't be surprising to find evidence of there having been movement inside the coffin, should one have reason to open it again at a later date. Although still a rare event even in the dim and distant past, these fears of premature interment led to some wonderfully weird inventions that, in theory at least, would save one from being entombed while still alive. In August 1868, Franz Vester of Newark in New Jersey took out a patent for what he called the 'Improved Burial-Case'. Vester's design included an air-inlet pipe, an escape ladder and a bell to ring for help. 'If too weak to ascend the ladder,' says Vester in the patent application, 'he can pull the cord in his hand, and ring the bell […] giving the desired alarm for help, and thus save himself from premature death by being buried alive.' Similar patents were still being granted to inventors in the late twentieth century, the fear of premature burial clearly still being deeply embedded into the human psyche.

A brief safety warning: if you did find yourself waking up in a coffin and managed to make enough noise that someone came to save you, it would perhaps be best not to pass judgement on your near-death experience. According to legend, Odran of Iona agreed to be buried alive under the foundations of a chapel being built on the Inner Hebridean Island in approximately AD 520. The hope was that human sacrifice would bring God's blessing to the site.

However sometime later, Odran allegedly poked his head up out of the ground and informed onlookers 'There is no Hell as you suppose, nor Heaven that people talk about'. Odrin's observation was rewarded with being promptly reburied on the grounds of heresy.

What precisely constitutes 'dead' is, to this day, open to conjecture. Lack of brain stem activity can be used as confirmation of death, but even this is sometimes fallible. 'Clinical death', the standard most often used to declare whether a person is dead or alive, is generally defined as being the cessation of both breathing and blood circulation. While this is a fairly logical and seemingly straightforward benchmark, each of these signifiers can and do sometimes cease temporarily – or become so faint as to be unmeasurable – for any number of reasons.

Modern medical technology has also muddied the waters of what it is to be really, truly, absolutely *dead*. Lack of brain stem activity is generally accepted to mean that the person concerned is deceased, but modern life-support machines can keep circulation and physical responses going. A person can be officially brain dead while still having a pulse and showing some physical reactions to certain stimuli. In some countries a person can be technically dead but still legally 'alive', simply because their next of kin have refused to accept the diagnosis on religious grounds (some branches of Judaism, for example, believe that death only occurs when the person is no longer breathing nor has a heartbeat). Death is still, in many ways, an ethical state of being as much as a physical one.

When Oscar Wilde died in Paris on 30 November 1900, his burial was hasty by any standards, his death having not been nearly so glamorous as many scholars would like us to believe. Wilde had succumbed to what was then known as cerebral meningitis, almost certainly caused by a severe inner-ear infection following a fall while in prison. His death was messy enough for it to be deemed necessary to add a layer of quicklime to his corpse, in the hope of accelerating decomposition. Unfortunately, the ability of quicklime to assist in the disposal of bodies has historically been rather overestimated – it is more likely to preserve a corpse than to destroy it (quicklime does, however, remove much of the smell associated with decomposition, which may be where the muddled myth has come from). After the traumatic drama of Wilde's death, one can only imagine his friends' shock when, on disinterring him nine years later in order to rebury him with more gravitas, his corpse was remarkably well preserved. In fact according to one witness, not only was he not looking quite as dead as they had expected, 'his teeth were lengthened'.

An earlier and perhaps even more tragic example is that of Elizabeth 'Lizzie' Siddal – model, muse and neglected wife of Pre-Raphaelite painter and poet, Dante Gabriel Rossetti. Seven years after his wife's death in 1862 (officially recorded as having been 'accidental', but almost certainly caused by an intentional overdose of laudanum), Rossetti was encouraged by his business-minded literary agent Charles Augustus Howell to have Lizzie disinterred from his family's vault in Highgate, north London. Rossetti had, in a fit of romanticism (or, more possibly, for reasons of self-obsessed guilt) placed the poetry that he had been working on at the time of her death into Lizzie's coffin, tucking it under her long red hair. Seeing his client suffering writer's block, Howell thought it would be financially advantageous to recover the poetry. Howell would go on to attempt to assuage his client's remorse over Lizzie's death by telling him that when he had opened her grave, not only had she not decomposed, but her hair had grown so long and lustrous that it now filled her coffin. This tale of romanticised tragedy led Rossetti to believe that Lizzie might actually be waiting for him in the afterlife. He left firm instructions that he was to buried eighty miles from Highgate, in Birchington-on-Sea in Kent, presumably to ensure he was at a safe distance from potential unearthly revenge.

There have always been myths about coffins having been opened only to discover that the body inside, rather than having become food for the local insect population, has somehow grown lustrous hair or has lengthy fingernails. Sadly for death-obsessed conspiracists, this is scientifically impossible. Hair and nails are 'dead' tissue – even when the person they are attached to is still alive – and cannot grow without a living host. What is possible, however, is for a certain amount of growth to *appear* to have taken place after death. Skin and soft tissue goes through a shrinking process as the corpse begins to dehydrate, which can give the impression that nails etc have indeed grown a small amount. Lack of decomposition can also be explained by fairly straightforward biological processes. Coffins are sometimes sealed to the point of being completely airtight, or are buried in heavy, clay soil. Either of these situations would slow the process of decomposition due to lower levels of bacterial activity and/or opportunity for animal and insect destruction.

Another potential source of supposedly 'undead' corpses is saponification – the development of adipocere, also known as 'corpse wax' or 'grave wax'. Caused by the anaerobic bacterial hydrolysis of body fats, saponification gives a corpse the appearance of roughly-cast wax, often with facial features still intact. More common in corpses with a high percentage of body fat, saponification prevents usual decay from taking place and might possibly be the scientific fact behind at least some tales of spooky corpse fiction.

In 1748, German writer Heinrich Ossenfelder published a poem titled *Der Vampire* ('The Vampire'), in which he tells the short but sharp tale of a rejected suitor:

> My dear young maiden clingeth
> Unbending. fast and firm
> To all the long-held teaching
> Of a mother ever true;
> As in vampires unmortal
> Folk on the Theyse's portal
> Heyduck-like* do believe.
> But my Christine thou dost dally,
> And wilt my loving parry
> Till I myself avenging
> To a vampire's health a-drinking
> Him toast in pale Tockay.
>
> And as softly thou art sleeping
> To thee shall I come creeping

---

* heyduck – foot-soldier (from the Hungarian *hajdúk*); 'Theyse' is the Tisza River in Hungary, which has its source in the Carpathian Mountains; Tokay (or Tokaji) is a type of Hungarian wine.

And thy life's blood drain away.
And so shalt thou be trembling
For thus shall I be kissing
And death's threshold thou' it be crossing
With fear, in my cold arms.
And last shall I thee question
Compared to such instruction
What are a mother's charms?

Ossenfelder's protagonist is portrayed as an aggressive would-be seducer who plans to take the girl into his deadly embrace whether or not it is welcome, believing it a far superior option in comparison to living within the boundaries of a strict mother. One of the earliest known portrayals of a vampire in modern literature, the poem is also one of the first times that vampirism is shown as having sexually charged overtones (potential implication of rape notwithstanding).

John Stagg was born in Cumberland, England, in 1770. A poet, he became known as 'the blind bard', having lost his sight in a childhood accident. Stagg's most renowned legacy is his poem *The Vampyre*, written in 1810, in which the protagonist is clearly yet to develop a sense of fashion to go with the fangs:

His jaws cadaverous were besmear'd
  With clott'd carnage o'er and o'er,
And all his horrid whole appear'd
  Distent, and fill'd with human gore!

Vampires as we know and love them today began rising from the grave only as recently as 1819, thanks to John William Polidori, the young physician employed as a personal attendant to Lord Byron. In 1816, Polidori accompanied Byron on a trip to Villa Diodati, the handsome house situated close to the southern shore of Lake Geneva which Byron had rented for the summer as an escape from the attention he had been receiving in England. Byron was at that time the hot topic of conversation in British society, thanks to his collapsing marriage and rumours of an affair with his half-sister. One can imagine that the opportunity to escape to a different country for several months was a tempting one.

Byron's close friends Mary Godstone and Percy Bysshe Shelley were themselves staying nearby, along with Mary's stepsister Claire Clairmont. Avoiding pressure from home themselves – Mary had already once become pregnant by Shelley (the baby was born eight weeks prematurely and survived for less than two weeks), who was at that point still a married man – the trio became regular visitors to the villa. 1816 was the year which would eventually become known as 'the year without a summer' – the 1815 eruption of Mount Tambora in the Dutch East Indies (now Indonesia) caused a catastrophic temperature drop, the ongoing effects of which killed millions around the world (it is now also suspected that at least some of the famously atmospheric paintings of J.M.W. Turner took their colour inspiration from the unusual weather patterns).

During a period of particularly inclement weather – Byron commented on it in his poem *Darkness*, 'Morn came and went – and came, and brought no day' – the five friends were compelled to take shelter together in the villa for three days, during which they entertained themselves by reading aloud from *Fantasmagoriana*, a collection of dark Germanic fairy tales. Inspired by this, the friends decided to hold a competition between themselves, in which each would attempt to write their own original ghost story.

The most famous result of this friendly literary rivalry was, of course, Godstone's *Frankenstein; or, The Modern Prometheus*, more commonly known simply as 'Frankenstein' and later published under Godstone's married name of Shelley. But Polidori would eventually prove to be a surprisingly adept competitor.

At the core of Polidori's tale was a fragment of a story – originally titled, rather literally, '*A Fragment...*' – that Byron had begun as his part of the competition but had grown tired of and left unfinished. The final story was all Polidori's, yet when it was published in the April 1819 edition of *New Monthly Magazine*, it was without either his permission or his name. Falsely attributed to Lord Byron, *The Vampyre* told the story of Lord Ruthven, who befriends a young man called Aubrey and proceeds to chomp his way through Aubrey's nearest and dearest. The pretence by Henry Colburn, editor of the magazine in which the story was published, of it having been written by Byron was reinforced by Polidori's use of the name Ruthven for the main character, Lady Caroline Lamb having used the name Clarence de

Ruthven for her thinly disguised portrayal of Byron in her 1816 novel, *Glenarvon*.

Despite the change to the supposed authorship having apparently been done without his knowledge, some scholars argue that it was in Polidori's interests not to correct the erroneous attribution, as Byron's name made for greater sales of his work. Regardless, Polidori certainly tried – unsuccessfully, at least initially – to argue that the work was his and had been unscrupulously attributed to Byron by Henry Colburn. Byron too was aggrieved to have been associated with the book, as he and Polidori had already parted on unfriendly terms. Contemporary anecdotes paint a picture of Polidori as a rather shallow and pathetic young man, intent on using the reflected glory of his employer to further his own literary career (his actual abilities as a physician being rather questionable).

What is clear from *The Vampyre* is that Polidori was already familiar with vampire mythology. Indeed, the introduction to his book references a 'credible account' of vampirism having taken place in the village of Madreyga in Hungary, involving a man by the name of 'Arnold Paul'. Despite the difference in location of the story – and it's worth noting here that the only references to Madreyga when one searches the web are quotes from said introduction – Polidori is clearly referencing the story from Serbia that was reported by Flückinger.

Lord Byron himself wrote one of the earliest literary descriptions of the vampire as we know it in English language text. *The Giaour* was printed in 1813, some six years before Polidori's *Vampyre*. In the introduction, Byron writes of vampiric tradition in what is now mostly Syria:

> The Vampire superstition is still general in the Levant. Honest Tournefort tells a long story about these 'Vroucolachas', as he calls them. The Romaic term is 'Vardoulacha'. I recollect a whole family being terrified by the scream of a child, which they imagined must proceed from such a visitation. The Greeks never mention the word without horror. I find that 'Broucolokas' is an old legitimate Hellenic appellation – the moderns, however, use the word I mention. The stories told in Hungary and Greece of these foul feeders are singular, and some of them most incredibly attested.

Variations on the undead bloodsuckers have existed for centuries, in almost all corners of the world. Byron talks of the 'Vroucholachas' – a creature of Greek origin whose name translates roughly to 'wolf hair', or werewolf, but which is undoubtedly vampiric in nature. More commonly known as Vrykolakas, Byron spoke of those in Slavic countries being terrified of such creatures and of such stories being particularly prevalent in Greece and Hungary.

A Vrykolakas is, according to myth, a rather mixed up creature, having characteristics of both werewolf and vampire. In Serbia and Bulgaria, however, the word 'vampir' was commonly used. Whatever the differences in etymology, the creature at the heart of the stories is very much what we would call a vampire.

In 1845, James Malcolm Rymer published the first instalment of *Varney the Vampire*. Sometimes attributed to Thomas Peckett Prest, the two men are often described as having been co-authors, although the evidence for this is dubious and the British Library lists only Rymer as the book's author. The first story to start bringing in those elements of vampirism so familiar to us today, such as sharpened, fang-like teeth, *Varney* was issued as a series of pamphlets in the style then known as the 'Penny Dreadful'. As the author was paid by the line, it is also an incredibly long (and presumably lucrative) tale. By the time it was published as a single book in 1847, *Varney* ran to over 650,000 words and even modern reissues come in at more than 800 pages in length.

Some of the tropes used through the series carry elements of other well known stories, including a chapter in which Varney is 'reanimated' using galvanism, presumably in a nod to Mary Shelley's *Frankenstein*.

Interestingly, across the course of the Rymer's epic fable, Varney becomes something of a sympathetic character despite his murderous tendencies – he definitely did not choose to be a creature of the night, fights against his animal instincts and eventually kills himself in order to escape his eternal fate.

The basics of modern vampire mythology – in literature, at least – began to be laid down more directly in Sheridan Le Fanu's *Carmilla*, published in 1872. Discussed more fully in the next chapter, *Carmilla* was originally serialised in the London literary magazine, *The Dark Blue*, from late 1871 to March 1872. The central character is emotionally and physically predatory, and prowls around at night, having apparently slept all day. Although the central tenet of vampires being 'night creatures' is a common one even in the early stories of revenants, by the nineteenth century we can clearly see a trope emerging, with vampiric characters becoming both more picky about their victims and also increasingly elegant in their methods of feeding.

In 1897, Abraham 'Bram' Stoker was working as business manager to Henry Irving, the renowned actor and theatre impresario. Married to Florence Balcombe (who had chosen Bram over her erstwhile childhood sweetheart, Oscar Wilde), Stoker supplemented his income by writing books, publishing ten novels and two novellas between 1875 and 1911. By far the most successful of these was *Dracula* (the other most well known of Stoker's titles is *Lair of the White Worm* – once included on a list of 'the worst horror novels of all time' and in which, according to writer H.P. Lovecraft, Stoker 'utterly ruins a magnificent idea by a development almost infantile').

Not only was *Dracula* by far and away Stoker's most successful work (although sadly for its author, it didn't actually earn a great deal until after his death), it would go on to become the most infamous of all the vampire tales. One could argue that pretty much all modern references to vampires owe at least something to Stoker's Count. He was the first to appear as a fully rounded personality with devious plans of his own (and morals to match). Stoker makes a richly detailed novel out of a story that, at heart, is quite simple – man loves woman, man must fight the attentions of another, possibly murderous, man for the love of said woman. It's *The Giaour*, but with the characters mixed up like a deck of playing cards.

Stoker was somewhat censorious and quite possibly intended *Dracula* as a metaphor for the perils of not adhering fully to what he considered acceptable social and moral values. Over the century or so since it was originally published, it has picked up the barnacles of critical analysis and opinion in much the same way as the Demeter piled up the corpses on its doomed trip into Whitby harbour. Some of the story's themes, however, are fairly clear. In Stoker's fantastical world of immortals, wolves, and people who can turn into bats, vampirism is portrayed almost as a form of communicable disease. This is particularly overt after the Count has landed in Victorian Britain. England of the fin de siecle had, in some social circles at least, become rather louche. Stoker had seen his good friend Oscar Wilde sentenced to prison for the crime of being attracted to men – something that must have caused Stoker some personal conflict, as he fought between his desire to support his friend and his wish to stay on the 'right' side of public morals. The 'New Woman' was making her appearance in society, having been brought to public attention by Irish writer Sarah Grand in 1893, in an article titled *The New Aspect of the Woman Question*, which covered, among other things, the double-standard of requiring women to be sexually virtuous while men were not. The question of female virtue is illustrated clearly in Stoker's invention of Lucy Westenra as a 'modern' woman who ends up paying for her sexual freeness with her life.

While it can be fascinating to analyse Stoker's characters and pick apart the many potential secret meanings within the details of the story, it's worth remembering that we are only ever putting our own spin onto someone else's idea. We don't know exactly what – if anything – Stoker was trying to say when he wrote *Dracula*. He may not have intended to say anything other than what is specifically on the page. What is certain, however, is that the Count has grown into the spine upon which the vast majority of vampire mythology hangs. This isn't surprising, of course – *Dracula* is literally the foundation stone upon which the vast majority of vampire storytelling has since been built. It isn't the greatest story ever told – in fact it is undeniably boring in places, its epistolary format clunky and overwrought – but within it lives the heart of darkness which powers all that comes after.

*Dracula* distils the various myths and leaves us with the essence of vampire. It doesn't matter whether other vampire stories have female lead characters, if they are set in the modern world or that of the Middle Ages; whether their protagonist is an all-powerful undead being with supernatural good looks, or a monster who hides in the shadows from those who would kill them is irrelevant. Regardless of the finer detail, the Count's bloodline runs through them all. But however important Polidori and Stoker might have been in the birthing of the vampire legend, the idea of the vampire clearly existed long before the bats first left the bell tower.

## Vampire Kryptonite

Garlic has long been believed to be a good 'purifier' of the blood and is to this day widely eaten for its supposed health benefits. The logical assumption is that, as vampires were considered 'impure' because they fed off blood, the addition of garlic to one's diet would presumably put a sneaky midnight visitor off his or her potential snack.

Porphyria is a disease which affects the skin and nervous system and is most famous for being the likely cause of the 'madness' of King George III in the early nineteenth century. Occurrence rates for porphyria differ around the world, but it is thought to affect less than a fifth of a single percent of the global population. Despite its rarity, porphyria was described by Hippocrates as early as 370 BC. The symptoms of porphyria can, in some cases, cause apparently vampiric symptoms in sufferers. Not only can it cause such extreme hyper-sensitivity to sunlight that skin blisters and burns, meaning that sufferers can only safely come out at night, it can also cause psychosis and turn urine red.

Sufferers of porphyria can also become overly sensitive to foodstuffs with a high sulphur content – which includes garlic. An even more unusual side effect of porphyria can be the desire to drink human blood, in much the same way that pregnant women sometimes develop pica, the desperate compulsion to eat substances that have no nutritional value and which would usually be unpalatable. Pica sometimes develops in response to the body's lack of a particular vitamin or mineral – stories abound of women eating chalk while pregnant, in a presumed attempt to up their calcium levels – but is more usually diagnosed when a patient is ingesting items that can have no dietary justification (and which in fact might be hazardous to health) such as soil or peeling paint. Similarly, blood would not have a directly beneficial effect on the person drinking it, but that doesn't mean the desire for it is any less 'real'. A lack of iron in the system might make someone crave the metallic tang of blood, even if they didn't understand quite why. Blood is, after all, a good source of iron, and would certainly help in a case of anaemia. This would all be marvellously relevant, if it wasn't for the fact that the vampiric side effects of porphyria have been largely debunked. Yes, it can – in theory – cause all of the symptoms listed above. But they do not occur often and certainly not with enough regularity to explain the endless cases of supposed vampirism over the centuries.

Crucifixes are a simple enough metaphor for those who have religious beliefs. God is the life, so it makes sense that He would terrify anyone (and anything) not committed to a good Christian way of living. As Christianity has been the major religion in the western world for most of recorded history, it's hardly surprising that its ethos and symbolism has been used as a force against supposed darkness since time immemorial. Both *The Vampyre* and *Dracula* were written by middle-class white men living in nineteenth-century England – it would have been more strange had their social background *not* had a huge effect on their portrayals of both the vampire itself and the things that threatened it.

We all read, watch and digest information through a filter brought about by our own personal beliefs and background. We then disseminate that information to others with our personal gloss laid over the top. All of history thus far is nothing more than endless grist to the rumour mill, each event being fractionally altered with every retelling and, over time, becoming something completely different. Facts and fiction are mixed, embroidered, distilled and re-presented as a new truth, even when we think we're simply passing on straightforward information. Fiction becomes fact if it's repeated enough.

This trope of fact becoming fiction was explored in the BBC's 2020s television adaptation of *Dracula*. Written by Mark Gatiss and Steven Moffat, this Count is darker, scarier and more undeniably evil than many of his predecessors – he also has, as I am fond of describing it, more issues than *Vogue*. As the three-part series goes on, we start to realise that this Dracula is far from the straightforwardly evil immortal we're introduced to in Stoker's original. This version is *troubled*. His is not the serene and careless existence one would expect from a man who is all-powerful and cannot die. He fetishizes the sun, demanding that the dying Jonathan Harker describe it to him, and sits mesmerised in front of the television in the house of another of his victims, watching the sunrise on the small screen. He cowers, screaming, from the cross as all vampires are expected to do and requires an invite before he can step over a threshold.

It is only in the very last scenes of the adaptation that we learn that all of these barriers exist only in Dracula's mind. He has spent centuries believing the myths (which in itself leads to some rather meta questions about where the myths came from, given that they were, in effect, invented by Sheridan le Fanu and then reinforced by Stoker). His fear of the cross is, however, absolutely real and immutable – and he knows exactly where it has come from.

While still living in his homeland, Dracula had no option but to feed on whoever was available. His diet was made up almost entirely of uneducated peasants who were in thrall to religion – they took the word of the Lord absolutely seriously, including that of the power of the

Cross. Absorbing their fears and beliefs for so long has left the Count himself vulnerable to religious symbolism – he knows it, hates it and understands that it is his weakness. As he says to Zoe Van Helsing when he finds himself in the present day, 'I can't *wait* to eat some atheists.' Zoe later argues her own version of his belief – that rather than having been 'infected' with the beliefs of the peasants he has killed, Dracula is purely and simply ashamed. Ashamed of his inability to face mortality head on and to 'die a true death'. But when we consider just how powerful a force religion can be when it comes to making people do what is perceived to be 'right', it becomes easier to understand that it doesn't matter whether the stories are true, so long as they are believed.

The earliest film interpretation of the vampire legend was F.W. Murnau's *Nosferatu: eine Symphonie des Grauens* (*Nosferatu: a Symphony of Horror*), released in 1922 (the Hungarian film Dracula's Death was released in 1921, but was so loose an adaptation that it is rarely mentioned in film histories). A thinly disguised retelling of Stoker's *Dracula,* Nosferatu was depicted as a repulsive monster, rather than the beautiful man he would become in later interpretations. Murnau had tried and failed to gain permission from the Stoker estate to adapt *Dracula*, Stoker's widow Florence Balcombe staying rigid in her stance that her late husband's work should not be changed in any way. He decided instead to play fast and loose with the details, in the hope of getting it past any copyright issues. This approach was unsuccessful – the film company filed for bankruptcy immediately after releasing the movie, in order to escape the lawsuit for breach of copyright that had been filed by Balcombe.

Murnau kept enough details to make it very clear to anyone who cared to look that *Nosferatu* was, indeed, simply *Dracula* by another name. The name 'nosferatu' was itself taken from Stoker's own words. As Van Helsing explains to his companions while they are preparing to kill the undead Lucy, 'Arthur, if you had met that kiss which you know of before poor Lucy die; or again last night when you open your arms to her, you would in time, when you had died, have become nosferatu, as they call it in Eastern Europe…'. Stoker was actually incorrect; although he took the word in apparently good faith from the work of nineteenth-century Scottish writer Emily Jerrard – and she in turn had taken it from an 1865 German-language work on Transylvanian customs by Wilhelm Schmidt – 'nosferatu' has no traceable Romanian etymology. It's thought that Stoker believed it to be Romanian for 'not dead', which in turn became corrupted to 'undead'. Perhaps the most likely source is a mistranslation of the Romanian 'nesuferit', meaning abominable, cursed or unbearable, depending on the context and who is translating it.

Murnau (who had changed his name from Plumpe, taking the name of a town near to Munich where he had once lived) bore some resemblance to a monster himself, standing at least 6ft 9in tall (some references have him as being nearer to 7ft) and in possession of a stern countenance. The German film industry was, at the time, one of the most productive in a world that had only just acquired the technology to make moving pictures. What there was a severe lack of, however, was the funds to make these movies look realistic. What could be more perfect, then, than a movie that was based on dark fantasy and therefore didn't need to resemble the real world. Murnau had long been interested in the German Expressionist movement, with its focus on creating emotion and sensation. The Expressionist movement had developed across central and Northern Europe during the first quarter of the twentieth century, and included such diverse creative fields as literature, dance, art and film.

As the German government had banned the import of foreign films in 1916, the country had no option but to produce its own. People were hungry for culture in a country that had been isolated by its involvement in the First World War and were looking for distraction. By the time that Germany lifted the ban on foreign films in 1921, its own industry was one of the biggest in the world.

Murnau's Expressionist take on the *Dracula* story is a product very much of its time. Dark and threatening in its setting, the titular character of *Nosferatu* is also nothing like the beautiful creatures of later years. Played by Max Schreck, Count Orlok is threatening in both attitude and countenance, with none of the erotic overtones that movie fans would come to expect of their vampires. Despite Murnau's alterations, *Nosferatu* is, to all intents and purposes, *Dracula*. The plot is simplified, not least because Murnau's cameraman, the acclaimed Fritz Arno Wagner, had use of only one camera. Despite the technical limitations, *Nosferatu* uses techniques that were advanced for the time, including a form of stop-motion animation which was used to make Orlok's coffin lid 'fly' back into place (the same technique is also employed in the scene where Orlok opens the ship's hatch as if by magic).

Stoker's family were eventually successful in their attempts to stymie Murnau. Prana-Film, the distribution company set up to create *Nosferatu,* was ordered by the courts to destroy all copies of the film. Thankfully for classic film history, one copy had already been distributed around the world and couldn't be recovered. All copies of *Nosferatu* ever since therefore owe their existence to this single escapee from the legal net.

Dracula's public image – and the one that would influence the media portrayal of vampires more than anything else – was firmly established with Tod Browning's 1931 adaptation, starring Hungarian-American actor Bela Lugosi as the titular Count. Some details are changed – Mina is Dr Seward's daughter and it's Renfield, rather than Jonathan Harker, who travels to Castle Dracula and has to make his escape. But the storyline remains roughly the same and Lugosi is compelling as the murderous, doomed Count. Having played the role on Broadway, Lugosi was determined to make the move to the silver screen. Despite opposition from studio executives, Lugosi got himself the part – probably due in no small part to him having agreed to accept a massively reduced fee for playing the role. Lugosi is now considered by many to be the epitome of the classic vampire.

The first adaptation of Stoker's book to include audio, when *Dracula* was reissued in 1936, it had to be cut to meet the requirements of the censors. The Production Code (aka the 'Hays Code', named after Will H. Hays, then head of the Motion Picture Association of America), had come into effect in 1934 with all its moralising limitations, and the Count's death groans were considered too much for the delicate sensibilities of its potential audience. Also cut was an epilogue which cheerily warned the audience against treating these things as mere entertainment:

> Just a moment, ladies and gentlemen! A word before you go. We hope the memories of Dracula and Renfield won't give you bad dreams, so just a word of reassurance. When you get home tonight, and the lights have been turned out, and you are afraid to look behind the curtains – and you dread to see a face appear at the window – why, just pull yourself together and remember that after all, there *are* such things as vampires!

# Chapter Two

# For the Blood is the Life

'Vampires are total sexual metaphors; there's just no way around that.'

Alan Ball, creator *True Blood*

We have been attracted to vampires for as long as vampires have existed in the human consciousness. Sometimes that attraction is overtly sexual, at other times more akin to a small animal, frozen with fear in the sights of a bigger, faster predator. Vampires are visceral in a way that humans rarely are – they are animalistic and driven by primal instincts, rather than by manners and societal niceties. Vampires don't bother pretending to be human. They are both *of* us and also above us – in the food chain, at least. They are fangs and blood and sex and urges the like of which many of us would never even dare utter in our own minds, let alone aloud to another human. They mesmerise and seduce us via page and screen and we gaze, rapt, as they hunt us down like the pathetic little animals we are.

Unsurprisingly, Sigmund Freud, the grandfather of modern psychoanalysis, had plenty to say about vampires. His views on 'psychosexual stages' – oral, anal, phallic, latency and genital – have been well documented and argued over for a century now. Yet they are still interesting to anyone curious about what propels us as humans to fixate on different forms of physical connection. By his logic, those drawn to physical re-enactment of the vampire myth must be stuck at the oral stage, as though they are babies searching for their next comforting feed. The human psyche is such a complicated tangled web that it is unlikely we will ever establish precisely what compels some into acts which would repulse others, but we are all the more fascinating for it.

Marilyn Miller is a British psychoanalytical psychotherapist. I asked her what the world of psychotherapy makes of society's enduring addiction to the bloodsucking undead:

Interest in vampires has its roots in our archaic infant phantasy world. That inner world lives on inside of us as adults, and feeds and shapes our imagination, giving deeper and sometimes exotic meanings to everyday experience. Those residues of infant phantasy also drive the form and direction of our creative and cultural lives, including the world of Vampires.

Our primitive unconscious phantasy world develops in the first few weeks and months of life, before a separation between mental and physical experience has been established; before language is available and with it precision of thought. The imaginary world of the human infant is embodied (literally) in daily physical experiences that are experienced mentally and physically at the very same time, without the sophistication of language and grammar that allows us to organise and represent that experience. We are in the world of equations not representation. Hunger becomes sucking something dry or taking cannibalistic pleasure in a 'raid on the breast'.

Freud worked with children early in his professional life and gave us the developmental stages, associated with physical and mental development, referred to by the author above. He understood also how dreams carry in condensed and poetic forms our past and current history, and the earlier 'fixations' that cast light on the quirks and oddities of adult fears, repeated habits and sexual life. The equation of body and mind was rarely absent in these throwbacks to early body mind experience and imagination.

It took another group of British based psychoanalysts however, to chart in graphic detail the imaginary world of the human infant. Through direct work with young children in the form of play therapy (notably Klein and Isaacs), and thence for learning purposes, through the use of disciplined weekly observation of new-borns and young children (Bick), a new light was cast on the surprisingly sophisticated story telling capacity of very young children.

The work of this British School of psychoanalysts was revelatory and highly controversial. However (and this is often overlooked when their abstract theory is taken out of its first-hand origins) their accounts were based on direct evidence of what children actually said in therapy. The children's accounts of their play revealed the shocking way their primitive (or as yet uncivilised) instincts could give melodramatic and violent force to their seemingly 'innocent' story lines.

A world of blood and spitting, violent cannibalistic hunger, of burning and dropping bombs, and other cruelties was revealed. Not only that, these 'horror stories' were told with obvious pleasure and excitement. This seemingly playful set of storylines was also shaped by familiar bodily experiences: feeding (sucking and biting and spitting), and toileting (wrecking, spoiling, bombing, cutting and soiling). That their cruelty was patently pleasurable, and erotic (in the sense of full of vitality) – was a shocking revelation.

A particular focus of the child's storytelling was the imaginary relationship between the infant and the mother's body, which charted the pleasures and frustrations of a physical kind through daily routines of infant care. Sometimes a new pregnancy sensed when earlier the mother's body changed, or the smell of recent adult sexual activity found new dramatic expression. Fear, envy and rage followed. Sometimes the infant's hunger, left for too long, led rage to fill the gap.

From these elemental fragmented experiences, the primal phantasy life of the infant revealed through play therapy later in childhood, showed how later the adult too, is excited by the hunt and the kill, and can create exquisite narratives of exotic bloodsucking cruelty first and foremost experienced through the mouth.

Given society's obsession with humanising even the most degrading of traits and desires, it probably isn't all that surprising that what used to be called 'clinical vampirism' – the intentional ingestion of human blood – became known as 'Renfield Syndrome', after Stoker's hapless character in *Dracula*. Renfield is trying his best to become what he believes his 'master' requires and is maddened with his desperation to please.

He catches and eats first insects, and then other creatures of increasing size, clearly believing that their life force is transferred to his own body through his ingestion of their physical form. 'Renfield Syndrome' was first used in a clinical context in 1992 by psychologist Richard Noll, who didn't actually expect it to be taken seriously. He was, in effect, mocking the increasing use of trite names in the field of psychology – unfortunately for him, this particular name was so snappy that it caught on. It has been popping up in both academic papers and the mass media ever since.

While one can, perhaps, understand the possible connection between ingesting blood as an accident and it then combining with sexual urges in order to create a monstrous desire, Renfield Syndrome is in fact so rare that it is almost non-existent. Yes, there are those who have killed or injured another person and drunk their victim's blood, but these are almost invariably cases of psychological illness or sheer murderous intent. There are, certainly, some individuals who believe themselves to be 'true' vampires and who adopt the lifestyle habits to go with it. Every now and then a story pops up in the media about 'real' vamps – invariably very ordinary-looking people who live in the suburbs and take their role as creatures of the night very seriously indeed. Such articles are often illustrated with photographs of a couple dressed in black, sitting at the dining table and toasting each other with a glass of blood. Interestingly, there appears to be a hierarchy in the 'real vampire' world, with those who indulge their love of gothic fashion being looked down upon by blood drinkers who see their habits as nothing to get excited about. The more serious a 'real' vampire is about their life choices, the more likely it is that you could engage them in conversation without ever having the faintest idea that they're just heading home for a relaxing glass of O negative.

There are cultural and ethical rules to follow if one wishes to become a valued member of vampiric society. 'Real' vampires feed carefully from willing donors, rather than simply taking a victim from the streets. Said donors have their blood tested to avoid the spread of disease. And the community as a whole sees itself as a responsible social unit, looking out for each other as well as working towards persuading society that they are genuine in their intent, however strange it might seem to others. In this, vampirism can perhaps be compared to those in the kink/BDSM community. Practitioners of BDSM – bondage, discipline, dominance, submission, sadism, masochism – have long been frowned upon. Their desires are pathologised, labelled, and viewed as an aberration in comparison to 'normal' sexuality. It is only during more recent years that mainstream society has begun – very slowly – to accept that the human desire for sensory experiences doesn't always fit into a neat psychoanalytical box.

Perhaps our love of vampires is in itself a type of kink? A form of power play in which we as humans get to play the outwardly unwilling submissive who is, if truth be told, thoroughly excited by the situation. Many of the earlier vampire tales in the English language were written by those such as Polidori who had attended private boarding schools and were all too aware of the pain that could be inflicted – with no fear of retribution – by masters displeased by their young charges. No wonder, then, that some of these grew up with mixed feelings about pain and pleasure.

For modern readers and viewers, there is also the attraction of going back to a simpler time – one in which all that matters is life and death. One's mind is sharper and more focused when the only thing to worry about is which pathetic victim to choose next. With less to fear from the world around them, even modern vampires as portrayed in films and books are usually free of the worries that drag the rest of us down on a daily level. Being immortal frees one from the worries of paying bills or holding down a job; the assumption is that you've been around long enough to either amass a fortune of your own, or have inherited it from a succession of mortal companions. Although not unheard of, it's rare to see vampires portrayed as anything other than wealthy and charismatic, wafting round the houses of our dreams and perfectly dressed at all times. When *Fifty Shades of Grey* turned *Twilight*'s Edward Cullen from a high school vampire into a high-rolling businessman, his instinctive desires didn't abate in the slightest – he simply moved them directly into the Red Room. It's rather ironic that Edward had to be converted back into a mortal before he could really let his inner feelings flow.

Blood is, of course, the essential life force – if we lose our blood, we lose our lives. Giving blood is a selfless act in which we pass our strength on to those who are in greater need of it. Allowing someone – or something – to *take* our blood is an act of trust and intimacy. Even when carried out in a sterilised, white-painted blood donation centre, there is something almost primal about allowing another person to draw out our very essence, regardless of how clinical the conditions. Now transpose that situation into a rather more intimate one. Instead of sitting on a wipe-clean couch in a clinic, you are, instead, in close proximity to someone you find deeply physically and sexually attractive. When they move in for that romantic clinch, it is natural to offer one's neck. After all, it's one of the most sensitive parts of the body – the attentions of someone who is an adept neck-nibbler can be one of the most shiver-inducing feelings in existence.

The neck contains the jugular vein and is therefore one of the most vulnerable parts of the body. Predators 'go for the throat' precisely because it's the quickest and easiest way to bring down their prey. Baring one's throat can be the ultimate act of submissiveness, an idea which many find arousing.

John Payne's 1878 poem, *Lautrec*, references the vulnerability of the throat from the vampire's perspective (this particular vampire is the mortal Lautrec's female lover):

> And more especially my sight
> Sate on the glory of his throat:
> With fondling fingers I did note
> The part where it was left milkwhite
> And that whereon the full sun smote
>
> .....
>
> All suddenly, my parch'd lips clave
> To Lautrec's throat and in the scar.
> That did its fair perfection mar,
> So fiercely delved, that like a wave
> The bright blood spouted, fast and far,
>
> An arch of crimson.–Still he slept;
> For over all the night were strewn
> The curst enchantments of the moon:
> And as the hot blood through me swept,
> My sense shook off its leaden swoon
>
> And with parch'd throat I drank my fill
> Of that fell stream. Then, as I stay'd

My awful hunger, undismayed.
There rose within me higher still
That horrid gladness and there play'd

Full streams of fire through every vein.
The darkling majesty of Hell
Within my breast did surge and swell:
The infernal rapture brimm'd my brain
With ecstasy ineffable.

Despite seeming rather tame to modern eyes – and perhaps even clunky in places – Payne's lengthy work (at almost 200 stanzas long, it takes some dedication to get through it in its entirety) caused quite a stir at the time. Having been sent a review copy, Rossetti wrote to his friend William Davies, 'Do you know Mr. John Payne? And have you seen his tasteful Poem which is called Lautrec but might be called the Anatomy of Vampyrism? I have received a copy but couldn't read it for the horrors, and really don't know what to say to it.'

What is clear is that, even in the early days of what might be considered 'modern popular culture', the intimacy and power struggle involved in the exchange of bodily fluids was already being given quite some thought. Sex is power, and power is inevitably fought over. So when the two become entwined – or worse still, are in the possession of one's enemies – they provoke the strongest of reactions. The mere thought of someone else having sexual power can be intimidating to those who would oppose it. Through centuries of (mostly) patriarchal society, power has been fought for and held by men. So when women show that they too possess power, they are seen as a threat. Throughout long tranches of history, women have not been afforded the same education as that available to men. There has always been a sliver of fear running through the male section of society – a fear that if women were properly educated, they might just become a threat to male dominance.

Early female historical characters, such as Ancient Greece's Lamia, were portrayed as using their paranormal powers for acts of evil and were therefore despised. Even as society progressed through the Enlightenment, into the Industrial Age and on to the beginnings of 'modern' social awareness, women could only be seen to hold power if it suited men – and if it didn't, they were suitably punished. Sheridan Le Fanu's *Carmilla* might have been a strong, independent woman, but she doesn't engender sympathy in the way that Dracula does, or indeed Louis in *Interview With The Vampire* (and Louis was a massive cry-baby who needed a kick in the backside more than he needed a shoulder to cry on).

## The Blood Countess (who wasn't any such thing)

Countess Elizabeth Báthory de Ecséd (1560–1614) is often held as an example of truly evil, vampiric behaviour on the part of a woman. Whether she drank blood or not, insist the stories, she certainly murdered countless young women and bathed in their blood in order to keep herself youthful. The infamous story has everything – the wicked older woman whose vanity was such that she would murder youthful innocents rather than risk losing her looks – but it is almost certainly false.

A member of the ruling family of Transylvania as well as niece to the King of Lithuania-Poland, Báthory led an uneventful life until she was well into her forties. Having married Hungarian nobleman Count Ferencz Nádasdy when she was 15, the couple moved to Čachtice Castle in Slovakia – a wedding gift to Elizabeth from Ferencz and the Nádasdy family – and had four children (or three, or five, depending on which accounts you read). Count Ferencz appears to have trusted his wife's opinions and advice rather more than was usual for the time. Elizabeth was highly educated and her family one of the oldest and richest in the region. When the couple married, Ferencz agreed to take his wife's maiden name as it was considered more illustrious than his own. While her husband was away fighting in the Long Turkish War (a land war involving the Principalities of Wallachia, Transylvania and Moldavia, which began in 1593), Elizabeth was made responsible for the defence of her husband's estates. This was quite some task, as the properties lay on the politically important route to Vienna and had previously been plundered by the Ottomans. Báthory clearly took her role seriously, taking on responsibility for the welfare of those living within her jurisdiction. Anecdotal evidence shows that she personally intervened in several specific cases regarding destitute women, including one incident in which Báthory took up the case of a woman whose daughter had been raped and impregnated.

After her husband's death in battle – rather ironically he didn't die *because* of the battle, he simply dropped dead during it from an unknown illness – Countess Elizabeth Báthory was one of the richest and most powerful people in the entire region. Note – one of the most powerful of *all* people, not just women. This made some people uncomfortable, to say the least. Elizabeth's cousin Gabor had an eye on the throne and had he formed an alliance with his rich and powerful relative, would have been a major threat to those who would also wish to take power. The simplest way to stop this happening was to take out Elizabeth, a task taken on with great gusto by György Thurzó de Bethlenfalva, fervent Lutheran and Palatine of Hungary.

Accusations against the countess were nothing new – there had been rumours circulating about her behaviour since the early 1600s. Some of these were almost certainly based on kernels of truth – no one gains or holds power of that magnitude without having to fight for it, least of all a woman living in a staunchly patriarchal society. Elizabeth definitely wasn't a pushover and, with hundreds of servants to organise and land and property to maintain, one can only assume that some of her control came via threats and violence. Even so, the stories that began to take hold after Ferencz's death were extreme by any standards. Tales were told of servants being beaten until they died from loss of blood, people having flesh sliced from their buttocks before being forced to cook and eat it, and of some unfortunates having their lips and tongues sewn up. The most famous legend of all is, of course, that Elizabeth Báthory had young girls and women murdered in order for her to bathe in their blood as some form of mediaeval skincare regime.

The only 'proof' for any of these stories were accusations made by Elizabeth's closest staff, almost all of whom were tortured into giving their confessions. This paper-thin 'evidence' was enough for Thurzo, however, who simply rode roughshod over the justice process. After accusing Bathory of being caught red-handed committing said appalling crimes (no real evidence was ever produced), he held a trial during which the accused was not allowed to speak in her own defence. Some form of political power-play was clearly still in force, because Elizabeth, rather than being executed, was locked up in her own castle, where she died four years later.

As for the 'bathing in virgin's blood' legend? Sadly for the historical conspiracists, it is so unlikely as to be pretty much impossible.

Apart from the sheer manpower required to kill and drain enough people to fill even the shallowest of baths, blood coagulates rapidly and unevenly. Elizabeth, had she even attempted such an act, would have found herself sitting in an unpleasantly cold and lumpy soup of stinking bodily fluids that probably carried diseases. One short dip would have been enough to make anyone decide against such extreme anti-ageing treatments.

Báthory is an example of political machinations leading to levels of group-think that risk turning to hysteria. In an era of little legal protection, women in particular were at risk of being used as pawns in political games, with no care for their personal safety. A woman with a strong will was terrifying, and a woman whose husband trusted that will even more so.

'Mina ... drink, and join me in eternal life....' Regardless of your feelings about the somewhat wooden acting elsewhere in the film, the scene in *Bram Stoker's Dracula* in which Gary Oldman's Dracula invites Mina Murray to join with him for eternity surely has to be one of the most beautifully sensuous depictions of the myth ever committed to film. In comparison to the original literary character (despite the title, Coppola's adaptation is far from being true to Stoker's original vision), Winona Ryder's Mina is a more than willing participant, licking the blood from the Count's chest even as he realises he cannot inflict eternity on the woman he loves so deeply. As he pushes her away, she begs, 'Please, I don't care ... make me yours....' Wrestling his innate animal instincts, he tells her he cannot allow her to become cursed as he is, but we can see her fighting to have her way. Her line 'Take me away ... from all this ... death,' before she forces herself back onto him surely has to be up there with the classics.

Despite both characters still being (almost) fully clothed, this is as hot as any full-on sex scene, the raw passion and desperate need practically coming off the screen in waves. Even though their tryst is broken up by Van Helsing et al, the fact that Mina has ingested the vampire's blood means that she is now connected to him in a psychic and almost spiritual way. This is used by our Victorian version of the Scooby gang – in the form of Van Helsing, Harker, Quincy and Holmwood – to hunt Dracula back to his lair within the crumbling castle. This adaptation relies on its early 'prequel' scenes to imply that Mina is the reincarnation of the Count's lost love, a plot device which doesn't exist in the original. Coppola's version pushes the 'fated lovers' angle to the max, with Dracula and Mina/Elisabeta portrayed as the epitome of perfect-yet-doomed love, which no man shall tear asunder (in the original, Mina simply becomes the focus of Dracula's misplaced obsession). When Mina takes dinner and drinks absinthe with her 'Prince', the fairy-tale powers of the green fairy become almost literal, Elisabeta rising up in her eternal memories and enabling Mina to feel her emotions across the centuries.

A similar kind of 'blood tie' is used as the central thread of the love/hate relationship between Dracula and Sister Agatha/Zoe Van Helsing in the 2020 BBC television adaptation of the story. Already clearly fascinated by each other, Dracula literally takes Agatha inside himself, both physically and mentally, when he drinks her blood. She goads him into biting her, muttering, 'Come – suckle, boy', as he prepares to pounce. Before he finally drinks, he talks of taking her with him wherever he travels and we know that he means by the power of her blood, rather than as a living, breathing companion.

Sister Agatha, the most cynical and scientifically curious nun you could ever hope to meet, knows only too well the power contained within blood. When she is discovered hidden away in a cabin during the fated trip on the *Demeter* and used as a scapegoat by Dracula in an attempt to hide his true identity, she finds the strength to goad him yet again by biting her lip and spitting her own blood at him. Agatha isn't scared to use the most powerful weapon she has. Her connection with the Count is such that when her descendent, the terminally ill Zoe, drinks Dracula's blood after taking samples in her rather gothic laboratory, the circle is complete. Memories, sensations and emotions now have a clear run through the centuries and through Zoe's mind, in much the same way that Elisabeta rises up within Mina Murray. As Zoe weakens, Agatha props her up from inside, her fascination with the Count keeping her great-great-niece going until the situation reaches its inevitable end, whether Zoe likes it or not. By the time we reach the denouement – Zoe and Dracula alone in a modern penthouse, with nothing but a table and centuries of pent up angst between them – the modern scientist and the centuries-dead nun are all but the same person. We might be looking at Zoe, but she snaps back and forth between herself and Agatha as her life ebbs away, the boundaries weakening between the different worlds in which her blood exists.

It's Agatha who finally discovers Dracula's true weakness, but she couldn't have done it without Zoe. And the Count is more physically and mentally tied to both women than he would ever like to admit. His decision to drink Zoe's blood in order to transport her spiritual form to a kinder, less painful end is not entirely altruistic – by doing so, he takes himself there with her. For the first time since his transformation into the king of all bloodsuckers, Dracula is not alone.

# Chapter Three

# Attack of the Jazz Vampires

Over the centuries, our expectations of what, precisely, a vampire 'is' has homogenised, its clarity picking up speed during the last 150 years – first with the growing popularity of mass-market paperbacks and then with advent of movies. We expect our vampires to be dark in aesthetic and delicious with the scent of temptation. They should be evil, but delectably so – and with an air of vulnerability, in order for us to convince ourselves that they might actually turn out to be good after all. Perhaps they just need the love of a good human man or woman.

We know that we can check someone for vampire tendencies by sneaking a peek in the mirror, in order to ascertain whether or not they have a reflection. If we're feeling a bit insecure, we can just add a bit extra garlic to our dinner and carry on in the confidence that it will ward off any stray neck-munchers. And surely no vampire would dare ignore a crucifix being waved in their face? Of course, the power of the cross as an anti-vamp safety measure depends first on your attacker knowing that they're supposed to be scared of it, and secondly believing the myth enough to actually buy into it. As we shall see, many interpretations of the vampire legend have, over the years played extremely fast and loose with these 'rules'. I'm sure that many a crucifix-resistant vamp is tucking into their garlicky dinner as I type.

The baobhan sith – pronounced *baa'van see* – walks the darkest corners of the Scottish countryside on deer hooves instead of feet, which she keeps covered with a long green dress. Traditional Scottish lore has it that, should one make a wish at night, then God's protection should also be requested. For if it isn't, the wish will almost certainly come true – but bring terrible consequences along with it. Probably the best known of the baobhan sith stories is that recorded by renowned Scottish folklorist Donald Alexander Mackenzie in his book *Scottish Folklore and Folk Life*, published in 1935. He tells of a group of men who, after a day's hunting, take shelter in a shieling – a type of small hut or building commonly dotted around bleak areas at the time. The four men passed the time by singing and dancing, with those who were dancing expressing a wish that they had partners. As soon as the desire was uttered, four women entered the shieling. Three of them danced with the men, while the fourth sat with the singer. One of the men, realising that blood was dripping from his companions, made a panicked escape and was chased by his would-be paramour. He managed to get to a nearby field of horses, at which point the woman became powerless to harm him, apparently repelled by the equine presence. When daylight came, he returned to the shieling and discovered his companions dead – 'the creatures with whom they had associated had sucked the blood from their bodies'.

Another story has hunters taking refuge in a cave, with all bar one saying that he wished his sweetheart were there with him. This was the cue for the baobhan sith to make their gleefully murderous entrance. The only survivor of the subsequent attack was a man called Macphee, who had his dog with him for protection and had declared that he was happy his wife was in her own house. The dog drove the women from the cave and fought off a 'great hand' which thrust itself in through the entrance, groping for Macphee. Sometimes described as a form of fairy, the baobhan sith are, as with many other folk tales, similar in presentation to the legend of the succubus, With the finer details merely adapted to each cultural and geographic location, the simultaneously seductive and murderous woman has existed in the human mindset for millennia.

Despite Mary Shelley's *Frankenstein* being by far the better known product of Byron et al's 1816 Swiss vacation, Polidori's *The Vampyre* pretty much set the template for western vampire legends from then on. Gone were the ragged shrouds and ugly features, replaced by devilishly handsome upper-class men wearing formal suits and sharp smiles. But it wasn't always men. Always the outsiders, vampires have often been used as a trope to illustrate topics that would otherwise have struggled to be accepted in polite society. Sheridan Le Fanu's *Carmilla* was just such a story. The eponymous tale of a predatory young woman, Carmilla is, by rather convoluted means, left to stay at the home of a widow and his daughter. The kindly – if rather gullible – pair have no idea of their new lodger's background. Carmilla becomes very close to Laura, the young lady of the house and Laura is grateful for the companionship, her closest friend having died under mysterious circumstances. There is an air of romantically entwined fate about the story from the start, Carmilla and Laura having recognised each other immediately from a dream both girls had in their childhood. The young women's connection is further reinforced by the delivery of a painting that had been away for restoration – a portrait of Laura's ancestor Mircalla, the image bears a striking resemblance to Carmilla.

Carmilla proves to be a rather high-maintenance house guest. Sleeping through the day, she spends each night apparently sleepwalking and occasionally makes romantic overtures towards Laura. Carmilla also avoids joining the family in their prayers, which in the early nineteenth-century was in itself considered to be a large black mark against a person's character.

Laura and her father go on a trip without Carmilla (who is, of course, asleep when they leave, it being daytime), and meet up with General Spielsdorf, uncle of Laura's late friend Bertha. He explains the circumstances of Bertha's death and that how, just before she met her fate, she had befriended a young woman by the name of Millarca. Not only is her name an anagram of Carmilla, she arrived in almost identical circumstances to those in which Carmilla had come to live with Laura and her father. Realising that Carmilla, Millarca and Mircalla are all one and the same, the trio travel on to the nearby town of Karnstein together in order to locate Mircalla's tomb, in order that the General might put an end to her forever. Carmilla appears when the General and Laura are alone and, flying into a rage, once again manages to avoid the General's attempts to kill her. The group is eventually joined by Baron Vordenburg, who finally destroys the vampiric Mircalla.

Carmilla was an openly gay woman long before lesbianism was regularly acknowledged in public. Regardless of whether the psychoanalytical angle of 'girl-on-girl = evil' was intentional, one can only hypothesise. But same-sex relationships were certainly far from being socially acceptable during the nineteenth century, giving such stories added power to both horrify and titillate the thrill-seeking Victorian reader.

More recently, vampires have been given the literary freedom to be pretty much whatever we want them to be and there are endless examples of modern portrayals in which the bloodsucking characters are far from traditional. Vampires can be the good guys as well as the bad, and we love nothing more than to think that they might actually be around us already, without us knowing.

Just occasionally, however, they come flouncing extravagantly out of the coffin. In *True Blood*, Charlaine Harris's depiction of modern-day vampires living openly in small town Louisiana is lifted from its original home in the Sookie Stackhouse series of novels and brought to shiny, sharp-fanged life on the small screen. Our heroine is a telepathic waitress who becomes romantically entangled with Bill Compton, the new vampire in town. It's worth noting that the television adaptation is far more visceral than the relatively light-hearted book version – blood literally takes its place centre stage as the star of this show. These vampires are out of the coffin and they want equality. Having spent centuries hiding in the shadows and feared by all, the invention of the synthetic 'Tru Blood' blood substitute means that – in theory, at least – humans can now feel safe in vampire company. But can vampires ever really be 'safe'? In Harris's world, vampires have existed parallel to humans for millennia, feeding and killing and hiding away to avoid becoming targets themselves. Is putting them on a pseudo-vegetarian diet really going to break the habits of eternal lifetimes?

It's perhaps more useful to compare the themes in *True Blood* with civil rights movements, particularly those of the LGBT+ community. Some of the phrases used in the series – 'coming out of the coffin', 'God Hates Fangs' – are adapted directly from those used on both sides of the fight for gay rights. Whatever the specifics, *True Blood* is hot on minority rights – everyone deserves equality, even those who have to sleep in shallow graves during daylight hours.

Despite being a mere mortal (at least, that's what we're led to believe at the start of the series), Sookie is not prepared to be treated as a walking buffet by the animalistic vampires with whom she becomes involved. She might be what she would herself describe as 'a lady' and have the quiet manners to match, but Sookie has a core of pure steel and isn't going to allow herself to be taken advantage of, however attractive her fanged suitor might be. An outsider all her life because of the telepathic abilities that mean she can listen in on people's thoughts, Sookie has grown used to keeping herself to herself. She certainly doesn't expect to ever meet a man who can cope with the intrusive nature of her abilities. Then Bill Compton walks into her life. What becomes clear very quickly is that Sookie is not going to be the pushover that either Bill or his cohorts have grown to expect from humans. She is unaffected by 'glamour' and is so used to being suspicious of other people's motives that she isn't going to allow herself to be led astray by the first pretty vampire who comes along.

What we're left with is the story of how kindness doesn't necessarily equate to weakness and that the quietest, most unassuming of people can turn out to be the most brave. There is a power in Sookie's unassuming nature that fascinates those around her and makes her irresistible to those who would both seduce her and those who would kill her (and some who would like to do both).

Oskar Eriksson is a 12-year-old-boy who lives with his mother in Blacksburg, a suburb of Stockholm. Oskar's new neighbour Eli seems different in a way that appeals to the lonely and isolated Oskar, who collects newspaper clippings about murders and sits alone in the snow in the dilapidated children's playground outside his apartment block. *Let The Right One In* (John Ajvide Lindqvist, 2004 (adapted as a movie by Tomas Alfredson, 2008)) is heavy in its themes but light in its careful treatment of the fragility of feelings and of life itself. Lindqvist took the title from a Morrisey song, 'Let The Right One Slip In', referencing the supposed need to invite a vampire over the threshold before they can enter. The bullied and lonely Oskar finds a kindred spirit in Eli, who initially appears to be a girl of around the same age. As their friendship deepens, Oskar discovers that Eli is, in fact, a boy who was castrated and turned into a vampire over two centuries previously. Eli lives with a middle-aged man called Håkan who kills in order for Eli to feed – Eli pays Håkan for his 'work', despite it being clear that the older man is doing it for love. The paedophilic element of *Let The Right One In* is overt, yet Eli is nothing but pragmatic about the relationship between himself and Håkan.

Eli's straightforward approach to pretty much everything is never more apparent than when Oskar is attacked in a swimming pool and nearly drowns. The furious vampire launches into the water and rips his friend's assailants' heads off with his bare hands, his sudden appearance making witnesses describe it as being as though Oskar had been rescued by an angel.

And Eli *is* Oskar's angel. The two boys – so different in their backgrounds, yet so similar in emotions – save each other, in different ways. They care for each other in a way that neither has experienced before, with absolute acceptance and no deceit.

The sequel to Oskar and Eli's story, included in Lindqvist's eponymously-titled collection *Let The Old Dreams Die*, isn't really a sequel at all. We don't get the happy ending we're waiting for, or, for that matter, any clear conclusion at all. In Lindqvist's version of the age-old myth, vampires exist around us – and they might just be children. But is a 200-year-old child still a child? They might remain young in a physical sense, but their mental capacity and experience is more than the majority of fully grown adults. Eli (and later, Lindqvist implies, Oskar) presents as a physical child blended with an intellectual adult, and the result is an uncomfortable one.

A rather neat subversion of the standard vampire trope is displayed in E. Elias Merhige's *Shadow of the Vampire*, released in December 2000. If you like your movies meta, then this is the bloodsucking tale for you. A fictionalised 'documentary' that purports to be reporting on the 1921 filming of *Nosferatu, A Symphony of Horror*, John Malkovich plays F.W. Murnau alongside Willem Dafoe as Max Schreck/Nosferatu. In order to heighten the effect of early filming conditions, *Shadow of the Vampire* is filmed using many of the early cinematic tricks that were common at the time *Nosferatu* itself was made. The story takes the theory that Max Schreck really *was* a vampire and runs with it. Schreck had proven himself to be so convincingly in his role as the Count that legends developed over the decades, insisting that only a true vampire could have played the role so well. Some insist that *Nosferatu* was Schreck's only movie appearance – which would add beautifully to the 'real vampire' theories, if only it wasn't for Schreck's well documented appearances in at least thirty films between 1920 and his death from a heart attack in 1936. In a nod to more modern interpretations of the Dracula story, the music that Malkovich's Murnau plays to his actors and crew in order to set the mood for filming is actually taken from the soundtrack of the 1979 adaptation – called, simply, *Dracula* – by John Badham, which starred Frank Langella and Laurence Olivier.

In *Shadow of the Vampire*, Schreck is truly a walking nightmare; a man whose presence unnerves everyone who comes into contact with him. Murnau is portrayed as a man whose artistic vision makes him single-minded to the point of negligence, caring more about 'his' film than the safety of his cast and crew. The technical details are all but identical to those from the filming of the real *Nosferatu*, making it something of an 'uncanny valley' of a movie. It helps that the casting is perfect. As well as the big names playing Murnau and Schreck, Eddie Izzard appears as Gustav von Wangenheim, who is in turn playing Thomas Hutter/Jonathan Harker (I did warn you that it was meta).

47

A well known English comedian might seem an unlikely choice to play a German actor from the 1920s, but anyone who has seen the original movie will know what an inspired choice it was. Izzard *is* von Wangenheim, mannerisms and all.

*Shadow of the Vampire* pulls no punches when it comes to shredding the reputations of those it portrays. Schreck is an animalistic creature of the night who has no real understanding of what's happening, while Murnau guides him as though Schreck is an affectionate pet panther that might turn on his master at any moment. Murnau will go to any lengths to get his film made; his determination making him blind to the damage being wreaked around him and ultimately stripping him of any ethics he may have started out with. Murnau sacrifices his terrified female lead on the altar of film-making and ends the film as the biggest monster of them all. Despite the schlock-horror air of the story in general, the film is played completely straight, with none of the comedic slyness that one might have expected from such a direct reinterpretation. Schreck's Nosferatu may have been the monstrous star turn, but it is Murnau himself who strikes the most fear into the viewer's heart.

> The little blonde girl who goes into a dark alley and gets killed in every horror movie. The idea of Buffy was to subvert that idea, that image, and create someone who was a hero where she had always been a victim.
>
> Joss Whedon, audio commentary, Buffy the Vampire Slayer, season one
>
> (Welcome to the Hellmouth' and 'The Harvest', 2001.)

One of the most simple yet most memorable reworkings of the vampire trope has to be *Buffy The Vampire Slayer*. Hugely popular from the minute it first hit television screens in 1997, *Buffy* was developed by writer Joss Whedon from his movie of the same name which was originally released in 1992. The titular character appears at first glance to be a straightforwardly cliched American high school student – she's pretty, blonde and she desperately wants to fit in with her new classmates. But fate has something different in mind for Buffy Anne Summers. She is the Slayer – the chosen one whose responsibility it is to keep vampires, demons and endless other supernatural creatures (including, in one memorable episode, a praying mantis disguised as a female supply teacher) from overwhelming the earth.

Buffy is the antithesis of the swooning female victim, dedicating her life to destroying vampires rather than being seduced by them. Reluctantly dropped into the role of Slayer at the age of 15, Buffy spends a long time fighting to bring some normality back to her life before finally accepting her destiny. Hers isn't a cut and dried campaign against bloodsuckers and other assorted monsters – Buffy sees the good and bad in everyone, including vampires. She even embarks on a relationship with Angel, a vampire who has been cursed to have a human soul after angering a rival clan. This brings with it remorse for his time as one of the most deadly and sadistic vampires in history, a remorse that he attempts to assuage by working as an ally to Buffy and her friends. His relationship with Buffy becomes romantic – unfortunately for him, when a night of intimacy between the two gives him a moment of 'pure happiness', it reignites the gypsy curse and he returns to his hellish former character.

> High school was a horror movie. A horror movie of humiliation and isolation and power and cruelty.
>
> Joss Whedon

Buffy isn't the hunted. She is the hunt*er* and you'd better remember it. Buffy has agency and for that reason alone she should be held aloft above the endless tedious portrayals of fragile women just sitting around waiting to be rescued by whichever version of Van Helsing the writer has decided she needs. A woman can't rescue herself, can she? Oh, but Buffy can – even if she doesn't always realise she's doing it. She even has a slightly helpless male sidekick in the form of Xander, who starts the series as a typical 'know everything while actually knowing nothing' teenage boy, but rapidly matures into someone who realises that Buffy is wiser than him and isn't scared to admit it. Buffy's *real* sidekick is, of course, Willow – a downtrodden geek who blossoms within the warmth of Buffy's friendship, even when that friendship drags her into darker and more dangerous situations than she could ever have imagined.

Does bloodsucking have to be involved in order for someone to be classified a vampire? Not always. Vampires feed off other people, but there are no set rules insisting that it has to be blood (or even that the vampire needs to come into direct physical contact with their victim).

Most of us will have heard the description 'emotional vampire' used for someone who seems to suck all the sympathy and empathy out of those around them. We all know instantly what is meant by the phrase. In the television adaptation of *What We Do In The Shadows*, the small-screen version of the film of the same name, Colin Robinson is an outwardly normal looking middle-aged office worker. But Colin Robinson (everyone uses his full name at all times) is secretly an 'energy vampire'. He feeds off the emotions of those he has either enraged or bored into a stupor, sucking their energy as he goes. Colin Robinson has the kind of mild-mannered demeanour that makes the average person want to smack him hard within minutes of meeting him. And it is this very inoffensiveness that is his secret weapon – he is so extraordinarily meek and mild that his mere presence winds others up into a fury without him even having to try.

> 'Life protects itself,' said Dr Walid. 'As far as I know, vampires are the only creatures that can take life, magic, whatever – directly from people.'

> From *Moon Over Soho*, by Ben Aaronovitch

The *Rivers of London* series by Ben Aaronovitch is famed for its wealth of unlikely supernatural characters, from the malevolent spirit of riot and rebellion in the form of Mr Punch, to otherworldly women with carnivorous vaginas. And of course this version of London has vampires, because what sort of self-respecting, bustling metropolis wouldn't?

Aaronovitch's books are heavy with vampiric references right from the start. Peter Grant – apprentice wizard at The Folly, that magical branch of the Met police that isn't discussed in polite company – often references Polidori and his (sadly fictional) reference book, *An Investigation of Unnatural Deaths in London in the Years 1768–1810*. In the first, eponymous, book of the series, Peter helps to destroy the lair of vampires who have drained all vestiges of life from everything around them (including the soil in the pot plants outside the house). In *Moon Over Soho*, the second book in the *Rivers* series, Grant investigates a series of unexplained deaths among the denizens of the Soho jazz scene, proposing the initially preposterous-sounding idea that the undead could gain their strength from music alone (so long as said music is of high enough quality, even the undead having some standards). Soho's jazz vampires don't bite – they simply absorb the life force of the musicians from which they feed.

Aaronovitch uses vampires as a deadly weapon in *Lies Sleeping*, book seven in the series. For reasons that are far too convoluted to explain here, Grant has to deal with a 'family sized tin of vampire' – a Quality Street tin's worth, to be precise. When it comes to disposing of the weapon – which is noticeably heavier than one would expect from its size, and jumps around as if it has a life of its own – Grant wonders for a second whether the contents of the tin are sentient, as it starts to bounce frantically with the apparent realisation that it is about to be destroyed. Could the latent spirit of something that is already undead actually have feelings? Regardless of the ethical dilemmas surrounding the entrapment of supernatural forces in a sweetie tin, the contents are terminally dangerous – when Peter knocks against it with his arm, it numbs him from wrist to elbow as the trapped vampire essence siphons off his magical powers. Aaronovitch distils the vampire threat down to a portable and deadly chemical weapon.

Vampires as a musical? It has happened – and it has been almost universally declared to be A Very Bad Thing.

'A promising new contender has arrived in a crowded pharmaceutical field. Joining the ranks of Ambien, Lunesta, Sonata and other prescription lullaby drugs is 'Lestat', the musical sleeping pill that opened last night at the Palace Theater,' wrote Ben Brantly in his scathing *New York Times* theatre review of Elton John and Bernie Taupin's musical project on 26 April, 2006.

*Lestat*, John's adaptation of Anne Rice's *Interview With The Vampire* was, according to Brantly, 'undignified' and 'stiff, sub-Heathcliffian'. He went on to describe the character of Armand as being played 'as a sustained hissy fit', urging theatre-goers to resist 'the soporific spell of this whinefest' by amusing themselves with the heavy-handed 'homosexuality as affliction' allegory that he felt was threaded through the doomed production. Reviews were almost universally negative, with Peter Marks of the *Washington Post* writing that, 'Lestat's contribution to art and equality is demonstrating that a gay vampire with a two-octave range can be just as dull as a straight one.' The most succinct opinion was perhaps from the *New York Post*, which titled its review simply, 'Bloody Awful'. Unsurprisingly, *Lestat* did not add a great deal to the fortunes of either John or Taupin, managing a mere nine weeks on Broadway before closing for good. An 'original cast recording' was made on 22 May 2006, but John announced soon afterwards that there was no plan to release it commercially. So if the kings of commercial productions couldn't make a vampire musical work, could anyone?

Frank Wildhorn's *Dracula, the Musical* was completely sold out on its opening night at the La Jolla Playhouse, California in 2001, but despite sticking closely to Stoker's original story, the show garnered mostly negative reviews when it moved to Broadway in 2004. The production was heavily revised before it went to Europe in order to better match Wildhorn's original plan. This new version of the show was a roaring success which at the time of writing was still being performed around the world.

Logic would have it that, given the popularity of both vampire stories and musicals in general, a project combining the two would be a guaranteed box office success. So why aren't we swimming in vampire musicals and singing bloody songs in theatres up and down the land? Perhaps the two tropes – bouncy, emotional musicals versus dark, sophisticated vamps – are just too far apart. Maybe their potential audiences are simply too different? Those who love vampires are generally – not always, but mostly – darker and quieter than their communal singing brethren. Perhaps it's the aesthetics that don't sit well together? There is something undignified about a vampire singing – and the only dancing one expects from a creature of the night is the sort that can be done in full evening dress, lit only by candelabra. Of course, this has been used to great comedic effect – but one would perhaps argue that it is then a comedy performance rather than specifically a vampire story. The two rarely seem to sit truly together.

The one exception to the 'no singing vampires' rule is possibly *Tanz Der Vampire*, the musical version of Roman Polanski's 1967 comedy horror movie, *The Fearless Vampire Killers*. With a score written by musical heavyweight Jim Steinman, best known for his work with Meatloaf, *Tanz Der Vampire* included new versions of such well known Steinman numbers as 'Total Eclipse of the Heart' (which had been a massive global hit for Welsh singer Bonnie Tyler in 1983) and a variety of melody lines and lyrics from songs originally performed by Meatloaf. Steinman explained his (re)use of the Tyler song as being logical in some ways – he had in fact originally titled it 'Vampires in Love', intending to include it in a musical based on the Nosferatu legend.

*Tanz Der Vampire* has proved hugely successful across Europe since its Austrian premiere in 1997 and is still touring to this day. However, as if to prove that nothing is immune from the curse of the musical, the version produced for the US market was beset with production issues from the start and flopped spectacularly. With its title anglicised to *Dance of the Vampires,* initial plans had been to bring in Roman Polanski as director. This was stymied due to the outstanding warrant for his arrest for drugging and raping a 13-year-old girl in 1977. Having fled to Europe to avoid defending himself in court and the associated threat of jail time, Polanski risked arrest and prosecution if he entered the United States. More problems were created with the casting of Michael Crawford in the primary role of Count von Krolock. What might have seemed, on the surface at least, to be the perfect combination of talent and box office draw, the reality turned out to be an added complication that the production could have done without. As well as pushing for a bigger personal deal than the show was likely to be able to sustain, Crawford – fearful of being typecast and determined that the role as the Count shouldn't be in any way similar to his most famous turn as the Phantom in *The Phantom of the Opera* – insisted on changes that made the character comedic rather than dramatic.

Despite even more logistical setbacks caused by the 9/11 terrorist attacks and subsequent travel disruption, *Dance of the Vampires* still looked – in theory, at least – to be a guaranteed success. Unfortunately the show was now beset with far too many powerful cooks attempting to stir the vampiric broth, and it descended into a theatrical mess. After a run of sixty-one previews – during which the official opening date was put back on two occasions – *Dance of the Vampires* finally opened on Broadway on 9 December 2002. Jim Steinman was noticeably absent from the premiere, later describing the production as a 'shit pile'. On 25 January 2003, after just fifty-six official performances, *Dance of the Vampires* closed for good, having made a rather impressive loss of $12 million.

Vampires as cute and cuddly 'fiends next door'? The 'outsiders in the neighbourhood' trope is one that has been used endlessly over the years, for many different reasons. Most often, stories in this genre are a metaphor for a heavier topic – racism is the most obvious example – but occasionally the outsiders really are just plain, well, *odd.*

Looking back for examples of vampiric light entertainment, one often thinks of *The Addams Family*, with Morticia Addams gliding around her family's creepily crumbling mansion house in perfectly glamorous full length black dresses. But however popular the Addams' were – and still are – with the viewing public, their particular powers or paranormal backgrounds are never explained. For all we know, Morticia might just be a Mama Goth with a penchant for slinky black frocks.

*The Munsters*, however, are an entirely different kettle of creepy fish. First broadcast in 1964 and running for two series until 1966 (there was also a one off special in 1965), *The Munsters* made its debut just after *The Addams Family* hit television screens, the two series having been written and produced at almost exactly the same time. Despite being entirely unconnected, the Addams Family are briefly mentioned in 'Lights, Camera, Munsters' - an episode of *The Munsters Today*, the sequel series that was filmed in colour and which aired on American television channels between 1988 and 1991.

There is no doubting who – or what – the Munsters are. Lily is a vampire, dressed in the styles that had become so familiar to those who had previously seen the Universal monster movies. As Universal were the original owners of the Munster franchise, the writers were free to use the designs and styles from its back catalogue. This also meant that Herman could actually *look* like the instantly recognisable version of Frankenstein's monster that we all know and love – a privilege not bestowed upon other interpretations of the character, as Universal owned the copyright to the makeup design.

Undead or not, Lily is still, at heart, a working-class wife and mother who loves her family even when they are driving her mad. She adores her bumbling husband Herman (Lily and Herman Munster are often claimed to be the first live action couple shown sharing a bed on television, but that honour actually belongs to the sitcom *Mary Kay and Johnny*, which ran for three years in the late 1940s). Lily's doting father is known to all as 'Grandpa Munster', but his full name is Count Vladimir Dracula, or Sam to his friends. Grandpa's age varies depending on which episode's explanation you watch, but his car, the Drag-U-La, carries his gravestone, the inscription of which reads 'born 1367 – ?'

The Munsters have all the human background of any suburban American family of the era, Grandpa in particular having a rather complicated relationship history. Having fallen for a succession of mortal women, he has been married 167 times, but is proud of the fact that he is still friends with all of them (and visits them regularly). Lily, the daughter of Grandpa's thirteenth wife (who apparently dies quite often and was absent for most of the 1960s, allowing him a period of bachelorhood) declares at one point that she had 'a whole mausoleum' full of brothers and sisters to play with as a child.

The Munsters are convinced that they are simply another average family just trying to get by. They don't realise that they are any different from their friends and neighbours, remaining almost blissfully ignorant of – or at most, slightly confused by – the surprised reactions of others. To themselves, they really *are* 'normal'. And in many ways, they are – Grandpa is certainly discriminated against on occasion, but it's usually because of his immigrant background, rather than any fear of the occult. If anyone is the odd Munster out it's Marilyn, Lily's niece. Marilyn has not a single paranormal bone in her human body and is convinced that she is the freak of the family. The Munsters really are the 'family next door' – kind and loving, with a tolerance of those who don't quite fit in.

Some vampire movies make no attempt at literary worthiness, however important their source material might have been. *Love At First Bite* (1979, dir. Stan Dragoti) stars George Hamilton as the most 'of its time' character you could ever wish to meet. Hamilton's Count Dracula opens with the line 'Children of the night! Shut up!' and from that moment on, the tone is set.

Dropped into the middle of 1970s New York City for reasons that are utterly irrelevant to the plot itself (in short, he has been overthrown by the Communist government of Romania and his castle sequestrated for the use of the national gymnastics team), the Count loses no time in discovering hotels, blood banks and nightclubs. In this, the loosest adaptation of the story you will ever find, the Mina Harker character is a vacant, shallow and brazenly promiscuous fashion model called Cindy. Of course, the Count falls instantly in love and in return, Cindy decides that life as a bat is better than living off the earnings of lustful men in the big city. The pair fly off into the sunset as the most puppet-like bats ever seen in a vampire movie, but to where isn't revealed. Presumably they're planning to go back to the castle and train as gymnasts.

From this description one would be forgiven for assuming that *Love At First Bite* must have tanked. It was, however, a roaring success – costing $3 million to make, as of 2014 it had made more than $43 million at the box office. Even the most generous of film critics would find it hard to deny that this is a film that utilises minimal acting skills and the cheapest of special effects techniques. The bats appear to have been made by a kindergarten craft group and Hamilton's accent alone deserves to be locked up for crimes against humanity. So why do people love it so much? Perhaps it's because *Love At First Bite* is so far removed from Stoker's origin as to be completely irrelevant to the vampire canon. Everything that would usually be viewed as potentially frightening is played for comedy. The Count himself is an almost pathetic figure, made humorous only by his over the top playboy demeanour and 'jolly foreigner' ignorance of the ways of the western world. The film pokes fun at communism, foreigners and female sexuality in a way that would probably have been seen as offensive even at the time of its release – but when it's presented as a joke, it is somehow more palatable.

In a similar vein is 1995's *Dracula: Dead and Loving It*, a film directed by Mel Brooks and starring everyone's favourite movie comedian, Leslie Neilson. Described as satire, fantasy or comedy horror, depending on where you read about it, it certainly aims straight for the jugular of the comedy market. Bats with human faces crash into windows and slide down the glass, their faces a picture of squashed surprise. This interpretation of Dracula is as overblown as you could ever imagine and his huge hairpiece – a spoof of Gary Oldman's 'old Dracula' from the 1992 Coppola version – is used as a running gag throughout the movie. The Count makes his appearance complete with ridiculous over-the-top hair, only to casually take it off and hand it to someone as if it was a hat, revealing Neilson's usual grey/white hair underneath.

However well Brooks knew his source material – and he clearly does, lampooning many well know variations on the theme such as Bela Lugosi, *The Fearless Vampire Killers* and the Hammer Films series, among others – it all has to be used for comedic effect. But can a vampire really ever be funny? Despite Leslie Neilson's impeccable comedy background in such movie classics as *Airplane!* and *The Naked Gun*, his role in *Dracula: Dead and Loving It* is nothing more than a hanger for the endless and terrible jokes that almost invariably fall flat. The old-fashioned humour fails to translate to a more modern viewing audience, leaving one feeling rather as though one had been watching a low budget 1970s comedy, rather than a film that was chock-full of household names and came out in the mid '90s. *Dracula: Dead and Loving It* currently has an approval rating of 11% on review aggregation website Rotten Tomatoes and made just under $11 million at the box office, against a budget of nearly three times that amount. Which suggests that I am not the only person to have issues with this dose of dark silliness.

Otto von Chriek is a talented iconographer who works for *The Ankh Morpork Times*. This being Terry Pratchett's Discworld (Otto makes his first appearance in *The Truth*, the twenty-fifth novel of the series), it should probably come as no surprise that Otto is somewhat ... otherworldly. He is, in fact, a Black Ribboner – a vampire who has joined the League of Temperance and sworn off blood. Discworld vampires are obsessive creatures who need a passion on which to focus if they are to stand any chance of keeping their pledge. Otto distracts himself from 'the b-word' (no one is allowed to say the word 'blood' in his hearing, for fear of stirring his thirst) by dedicating himself to the art of newspaper photography. The main drawback to this is Otto's tendency to collapse into a heap of dust when using his camera flash, which is created from sunlight stored by the salamander he uses as a light source.

Not one to be held back by his paranormal disabilities, Otto has devised a simple and practical solution. He wears a small vial of animal blood strung on a chain around his neck, which smashes as he hits the floor in a cloud of dust and reconstitutes him quickly enough that he can catch his camera before it hits the ground and thus carry on with his work.

One would think that a job involving sunlight would be the last thing a vampire would wish to risk, but Otto is *fascinated* by light. It is the one thing that can kill him and he is almost suicidally obsessed with it. He experiments with 'dark light', only to discover that the downside of using the light you find on the other side of darkness is that it doesn't always illuminate the present moment – sometimes it shows the past or the future, which can be somewhat disconcerting.

Otto (there are different theories about the origins of his name, which might be a play on words – 'ought to shriek' – or even possibly a nod to *Nosferatu*'s Max Schreck) knows that he makes humans nervous and so goes out of his way to make himself appear as harmless as possible. He does this by the simple expedient of dressing like a walking, talking vampire cliché. Otto is all about the capes and sharp suits, because he is well aware that people are rarely scared of someone who looks like a caricature. In this he is different to his fellow Black Ribboners, who generally go out of their way to not stand out in Ankh Morpork society. Everyone in the city knows who Otto is and they accept him in the same way that a small insular village in the 1960s might accept people from different cultures running the corner shop – with amiable tolerance, alongside barely disguised suspicions and prejudices. By living up to the racist caricatures, Otto actually blends in. People find themselves less unnerved by someone they can laugh at, and Otto is prepared to be patronised in return for being allowed to take his place in society.

Pratchett dots vampire myths here and there in other Discworld novels, often using the automatic human subservience to vampires as a metaphor for issues around class and social mobility. There's Maladict in *Monstrous Regiment*, who, in the tradition of Black Ribboners has transferred her desire for blood onto something else – in her case a coffee addiction. Lady Margolotta (*The Fifth Elephant, Unseen Academicals*) focuses on power as a blood-replacement and has a 'do they/don't they' relationship with Lord Vetinari, a quality vampiric lineage (she is noted as having a four-page entry in the *Almanack de Gothic*, the undead equivalent of *Debrett's Peerage*) and a penchant for black rubber clothing. Vampires on the Disc are almost invariably upper class, even if they are somewhat embarrassed at the fact, and Pratchett gleefully uses them as a litmus paper on which he shows up the embarrassing subservience of those around them.

Count von Count is a name that is instantly recognisable to anyone who grew up watching children's television from the 1970s onwards. The enthusiastic vampire and his often infuriating obsession with counting pretty much anything he sees has been a regular member of *Sesame Street's* puppet cast since 1972. Aesthetically riffing on Bela Lugosi's portrayal of Dracula, the Count (his full name is almost never used) likes to, well, count things. 'One, ah ah ah, two, ah ah ah...' the Count counts it all with a distinctly eastern European accent (having apparently grown up in the Carpathians).

It has been suggested that the Count's arithmomania (a formally recognised compulsion to count almost anything and everything) is a trait given to him as a nod towards old superstitions. Many cultures believed that scattering endless tiny objects such as seeds gave protection from supernatural entities – some say goblins and others witches, the specifics vary widely – who would be distracted from their nefarious plans by the compulsion to count every last item.

The Count lives, in true vampire style, in a dusty old castle that he shares with bats Grisha, Misha and Sasha, among others. He also has a cat and a pet octopus, and he likes to spend time playing both the violin and the pipe organ. The Count is a Muppet of culture, peppering his conversations with endless references that are unlikely to be picked up by children watching the show but make their parents squeak with glee. In order to really keep up appearances, the Count also has his own personal thundercloud, which follows him around and provides a dramatic burst of thunder and lightning at opportune moments.

Speaking to the BBC's *More or Less* radio programme in 2009, (Muppets always stay in character, even when it is their voice actor who is being interviewed), the Count confessed that his counting addiction had got him into trouble on more than one occasion. He told of the time that he had literally counted his chickens before they were hatched because he was planning to sell them, only for some disgruntled would-be chicken purchasers to find themselves unexpectedly in possession of turtles or alligators. There was also the time he was working as a lift operator and annoyed Kermit the Frog with his insistence on stopping at every single floor in order to count them all properly. So addicted is the Count to, well, counting, that when he alone with nothing around him he resorts to counting himself. One, ah ah ah…

Why do we insist on turning legendary bloodsucking demons into cutesy comedy and/or cartoon characters? Probably for the same reasons that we anthropomorphise pretty much anything – to make it less frightening. We love vampires and can't bear to think that maybe they really would just prefer to bite our heads off and slurp on the blood fountain. It's interesting to note that Count von Count started his puppetry life as a much more intimidating character. When he first appeared in the early 1970s, he would make his entrances and exist hidden behind his cloak *a la* Lugosi. He was also fond of a maniacal laugh – complete with crashing thunder as accompaniment – and he wasn't averse to controlling other characters through his powers of glamour/hypnosis. These traits were toned down for fear of scaring his young audience and it's pretty much impossible to take today's version of the Count seriously. How can you be scared of someone who likes to bounce around amiably counting his beloved bats and whose favourite time of day is 2.30 ('tooth-hurty')?

(For those who'd live to see the Count develop a bit more…bite, it's well worth looking up the animated comedy short *Sesame Street Meets Blade*, which appeared on the Adult Swim series *Robot Chicken* in 2014.

With cartoon blood and violence galore, it's the vampiric reboot you didn't know you needed).

Leslie Nielsen's turn as Dracula in *Dead and Loving It* isn't anything other than that which it sets out to be – old-fashioned slapstick comedy – but somehow it jars when vampires are being laughed at, rather than with. The Munsters are funny and loveable, but we know they are still paranormal creatures. We laugh *with* them, rather than at them. Pratchett's vampires work because they are still deeply layered characters with personal and emotional issues of their own, even when they are being ridiculous. Polanski's vampire hunter – and the vampire he hunts – are funny but still portrayed with affection. We might want our bloodsuckers to be less intimidating, but they lose their lustre if they themselves become the joke.

# Chapter Four

# My Immortal

Immortality as an erotic trope is as old as, well, eternity. What could be sexier than living forever as a beautiful, charismatic superior being who is both apart from and somehow above those around them?

The idea of never having to face death is a tempting one at the best of times. And if one is living in an era of death and disease, losing one's 'soul' might seem a reasonable price to pay in return for immortality. Knowing you could never die would give a feeling of huge power. We might not be scared of the process of dying itself – although most of us would prefer it to happen painlessly and peacefully after a long and fulfilling life (and preferably surrounded by those who love us) – but for many, the real motivating terror of ageing is simply running out of time.

Many of us panic our way through adult life, scared of missing out and terrified of getting old and dying before we've achieved everything we planned. All we can do is hope that we stay alive long enough to get that final promotion, bounce grandchildren on our knees and hopefully end our days peacefully and without too much pain. Having that finite span removed would mean being able to take as long as we liked on projects, go off on holiday for six months 'just because' and break up with the not-quite-perfect partner because another one will turn up in a decade or so and maybe this time it really will be *forever*.

The thought of being immortal is also utterly terrifying. In a completely unscientific experiment, I asked on social media whether, assuming one could stay mentally and physically as they are now, people would take the option of immortality. A few jumped at the chance – 'I think it could be a blast! The longer you live the shorter time seems, so imagine when you reach centuries or thousands of years old? What a buzz!', 'Yes. You'd just have to get used to death. And changing eyebrow fashions.' My favourite was probably, 'This one is easy for me, I'd live forever. Death is a thieving bastard and has no right getting involved.'

But the vast majority said no. 'If we lived forever, we'd have to fashion a whole new paradigm. So much – I'd even say all – art, literature, philosophy – is predicated on the fact that we are mortal. Being mortal gives us an impetus and in some cases, a break. I reckon we'd get bored.'

'Watching everyone and everything I ever know or love wither and die? That's a punishment, not a prize.'

Imagine knowing that you will outlive your own children, grandchildren, great children and onwards, until the end of time. Climate change wouldn't be a hypothesis for you, because whatever happens you'll be around to witness it. Dying planet, dotted with starving humans and depleted wildlife? Yours for the taking. Doesn't sound so tempting now, does it?

The perception of immortality as the opportunity to spend eternity as a glamorously young and virile specimen of humanity is almost always the default approach. What would be the point otherwise? Lucky, then, that most vampire traditions imbue their heroes with the ability to age, regress and change their general appearance at will. Fictional vampires – as opposed to the early interpretation of revenants, who are merely 'dead but not dead' – can have any ability they so choose. Because what's the point of being fictional if you can't make it work for you? In *Bram Stoker's Dracula*, our (anti)hero is a European nobleman who happily kills anyone who gets in the way of his plans. Count Dracula determinedly seduces the innocent Mina Murray in the belief that she is the reincarnation of the beloved wife he lost centuries earlier in tragic circumstances. The titular Count ages while living in lonely solitude in his Carpathian castle, but transforms himself into a handsome man in the prime of life for his trip to London and the campaign to win the heart of Mina Murray. But however kind and caring she might be, one can't imagine the beautiful and thoughtful Mina accepting the overtures of a man who is centuries old and looks it, desiccated skin stretching like crinkled tissue paper over his gnarled bones and rheumy eyes peering mournfully out of a pale, ghostly face. No, Mina deserves better. And so the Count becomes a vision of the perfect man, charmingly adept at conversation and conveniently placed to 'accidentally' bump into Miss Murray and set about charming her tightly corseted frock right off those delicate shoulders. Gary Oldman's portrayal of the lovelorn Count in Coppola's adaptation is heartbreakingly beautiful, his wiry and sexual younger Count counterpointed by his equally brilliant – yet ultimately more tragic – older Count, who has to be saved by Mina herself.

We are aware from the start that the Count's life has been one of endless hardship and tragedy. His is a never-ending quest to avenge his lost love Elisabeta and bring her back to him in the present day. Already a force to be reckoned with in life, in death his power is mesmerising, focused on nothing except the goal of making Mina his. Nothing will get in his way. But when he's finally in a position to make Mina his forever, Dracula finds that he can't quite bring himself to do it. Even as she begs him to take her with him into eternal life, he is struggling – possibly for the first time ever – with the ethics of inflicting the horrors of undeath on the one person he truly loves. He doesn't worry about it for too long, of course – he's a vampire, not a human man – but even Dracula is only too aware of the reality of what awaits beyond this mortal coil.

Anne Rice famously wrote *Interview With The Vampire* after the death of her young daughter, creating the character of Claudia as a form of immortal distraction from her own tragic loss. In the film version of the book, directed by Neil Jordan and released in 1995, Louis de Pointe du Lac is played by Brad Pitt as the eponymous vampire, who is interviewed by the initially sceptical journalist Daniel Molloy (Christian Slater; the part of Molloy was due to be played by Slater's long-time friend River Phoenix, who died just before filming began – Slater donated his earnings from the role to charities that Phoenix had supported).

Louis's human story is a tragic one – a widower at the age of 24, he is so racked with grief that he neglects his hitherto successful plantation and courts death, purposely putting himself in harm's way in the hope of joining his wife and child in the afterlife. Spotted as a potential ally by Lestat de Lioncourt (played by Tom Cruise in the film adaptation), Louis accepts Lestat's offer to turn him into a vampire, in the hope that it might give him an escape from his torment. Of course, this only serves to trap Louis into an eternity of misery, unable to use even death as an escape route from his pain. The powerplay between the two men is fascinating – Lestat exudes a bratty, privileged confidence, while barely bothering to hide his desperate loneliness and desire for company. Louis still has a level of empathy that repels him from attacking humans, but Lestat feels no such moral restriction. After Louis feeds from the orphaned Claudia in a moment of desperation, Lestat takes the opportunity to turn her into a vampire, presenting her to Louis as a gift. The child is a pawn in Lestat's personal politics, merely a token with which to bribe his friend to stay with him.

It is Claudia who proves to be the undoing of them all. An uncontrollable child, she remains physically immature even as she develops mentally. Kirsten Dunst was just 11 years old when she played the part of Claudia, and her portrayal of an adult woman in a confused and immortal child's body earned her a Golden Globe nomination for Best Supporting Actress in 1995. Dunst clearly had issues with being required to act as a woman when she herself was no such thing, saying at the time, 'I hated it so much because Brad was like my older brother on set and it's kind of like kissing your brother. It's weird because he's an older guy and I had to kiss him on the lips, so it was gross.' Dunst later doubled down on her comments. Looking back on her quotes about *Interview* as an adult for *Entertainment Tonight*, she said, 'Yeah, it was gross! I stand by that. It would have been so much creepier if an 11-year-old was like, "It was great." You'd be like, "There's something wrong with this child."'

Uncomfortable scenes aside, it is the very presence of Claudia that gives *Interview* its uneasy tone. In modern culture, vampires are generally depicted as being inherently sexual. The juxtaposition of an immortal mind in a prepubescent body is an uncomfortable one. But regardless of ethics, the fact remains that Claudia, as a character, *is* an adult woman who simply has the outward appearance of a child. As with Eli in *Let The Right One In*, Claudia is a walking dichotomy, an adult trapped within a child's body.

In the *Twilight* series, Bella Swan (presumably so-named in order to make us think of delicate swan necks just waiting to be bitten) is warned time and time again that becoming immortal risks her very soul. Edward Cullen – still an overgrown and petulant teenager, despite being more than 100 years old – openly informs her that he wants to kill her while consistently acting like a particularly bad tempered yet lovesick puppy. Despite all the warnings, the gloomiest person from here to Betelgeuse decides that it's a risk worth taking. What's the worst that could happen? To Bella's mopey mind, the constant and imminent threat of being murdered by her own boyfriend is worth it just for the privilege of dating the town's resident heartthrob.

Bella's death wish only increases in intensity as the saga lumbers on. She makes a unilateral decision to die in order that her unborn baby might live, and looks surprised when Edward points out that, actually, perhaps it would have been nice to discuss things first. However well-intentioned Bella might be, she lurches through the series like a lost sheep that's just looking for ways to get itself killed, suffering through years of stress and pain and heaping endless anguish onto her father, Charlie. Rather conveniently, Bella's mother Renee – who starts out very clingy – appears to lose interest in her daughter towards the end of the series, possibly because she got sick of listening to the whining. And all this just so Bella can stare in awe at her beautiful glittery husband for all eternity.

Of course, if one can never die then one can never meet one's maker – a handy trope for authors who place great store on the power of the fight between good and evil, heaven and hell. Regardless, even hell is apparently more appealing if everyone in it is incredibly handsome. If there is an aesthetically displeasing vampire in *Twilight*, I have yet to find it. Pretty much every single one of Stephanie Meyer's bloodsuckers appear to have been 'turned' in the prime of their lives. Even the modern Gothic Elders – in the form of the Volturi – are extremely well preserved, as well as being impeccably well-dressed. Of course, this all plays into the 'deadly *and* beautiful' trope, which is necessary for the story to work. Bella would presumably be far less eager to join the ranks of the undead if she had to do it as a decaying, flaky corpse. These vampires all look as though they shop at ASOS (and they definitely have an Amazon Prime account).

Meyer's description of vampire skin as being 'like diamonds' serves to reinforce the idea that her vamps are superior to pretty much everything. They believe themselves to be better than humans, while also determinedly fitting in with modern mortal society (regardless of how many times it requires them to graduate from high school). They must be getting *something* out of this strange situation, but what? Certainly not a food source. The Cullens are proudly 'vegetarian' in the loosest sense – vampires who feed from animals rather than people. Their restricted diet is looked upon with scorn by most of the other vamps of their acquaintance. One can only assume that they plan to spend eternity showing everyone just what good (and beautiful, don't forget beautiful) people they are.

For all its faults, *Twilight* is in the minority of vampire interpretations in that it attempts to bestow some level of humanity to its creatures.

The Cullens certainly don't always find it easy to avoid drinking human blood. Jasper Hale is the most recent addition to the Olympic coven and, despite an aversion to killing that came with him from life over into death, he struggles to cope with his animal instincts when around humans. This is something that Bella discovers for herself at her eighteenth birthday party, when a tiny paper cut on her hand leads to Jasper's determined attempt to eat her in place of the birthday cake.

As well as being attractive to look at, the *Twilight* vampires are invariably rich. At the beginning of the saga Bella is overwhelmingly intimidated by the sheer amount of tasteful wealth around her, but as we crawl towards the end of her human life, she has miraculously resigned herself to a life of luxury. Even a surprise honeymoon visit to the Cullen's private island is greeted with little more than a raised eyebrow. Bella's ethics are clearly weak in the face of eternal wealth and good shoes.

Of course, vampires would almost certainly be rich – it comes with the territory. If you're going to 'live' for eternity then you're going to have to learn to get by, or risk being forced to exist permanently in the shadows. And – at least, according to established literary tropes – vampires have a preference for glamour and luxury. When Jonathan Harker first meets Count Dracula, the undead nobleman is withered and ancient, hiding in dark corners to avoid revealing the true decaying horror of his appearance. His physical state isn't due to a lack of money, it's down to his restricted diet – and he has plans to change that. He's had a long time to build up his financial reserves and uses it to game-play his way to England. The Count is looking for a new and better life (for himself, rather than anyone around him). Centuries of isolation – while speeding the mental journey to psychosis – also provide the time and space to stretch one's knowledge and vocabulary. By the time of his arrival in London, Dracula is quite the urbane Renaissance man.

A similar transformation happens in Mark Gatiss and Steven Moffat's 2020 adaptation of Stoker's tale for the BBC. This version is absolutely the Count's story – Dracula is front and centre as opposed to being viewed through the filtered eyes of others, as happens in the original. This Count first appears as a lurking, stalking creature – as predatory as ever, but only too aware of his inability to blend in with society. Of course, he makes up for this rapidly and even when he is dropped into the modern world without warning, he is startled for only the briefest of moments. Within days, Dracula has mastered the internet and modern social etiquette. He has also re-established his fortune. And he does it all legally, quietly and with great politeness.

Part of the game Dracula plays with himself is to assimilate himself as neatly as possible into all manner of echelons of society – even when he making the biggest of entrances, he is unobtrusive and polite in his manner. This is a psychopath you could take to any social occasion – tea with your maiden aunt, a royal garden party – and be confident that he wouldn't embarrass you. Dracula has, above all else, impeccable manners.

John Mitchell is a Byron-esque figure who appears to be in his late twenties, but was actually born in 1893. The first character we meet in the television series *Being Human* (BBC TV, 2009–2013), Mitchell (he's always referred to as Mitchell rather than John) was played by Guy Flanagan in the pilot episode. But by the time the first full series was commissioned, he had been transformed into the brooding, curly haired and intense Irishman Aidan Turner, whose sex appeal could have been bottled and sold as a pheromone scent. Looking for a date but all the girls ignore you? Then L'eau d'Mitchell is the scent for you!

Mitchell might exude the essence of vampire, but he doesn't want to *be* one. Having been given no option but to allow himself to be changed in order to save the rest of his men when they are attacked during the First World War, Mitchell resents his own existence as much as he's picked the fruits of it along the way. He is a walking tragedy, a man who is torn between two worlds and will never fit in with either. Working as a hospital porter, Mitchell attempts to carefully walk the tightrope between existing both as a human and a vampire. He welcomes the stability that comes from developing a friendship with George Sands, possibly the most unlikely and unassuming werewolf the underworld has ever seen. Each wrestling with the difficulties that come from trying to fit into the outside world, they rent a house together in Bristol, only to discover that their new home has a third, unexpected occupant. Annie Sawyer is a similar age to Mitchell and George, but with one disadvantage – she is actually dead. The vampire and werewolf are the only people able to both see and interact with Annie's ghost, and the three rapidly become close friends.

In later series we see flashbacks of events in Mitchell's vampire life, during which he acts as coldly and cruelly as any bloodsucker you could ever fear to meet. Through it all, though, is a thread of compassion – a tiny lifeline of humanity to which Mitchell clings with all his might, terrified at the prospect of becoming a fully fledged monster. Despite his rock-god looks and sharp social skills, Mitchell makes it clear that 'living' as a vampire is not the fun the movies would make it out to be. He is isolated and lonely, even when surrounded by his flatmates. There are parts of him that he will never let them see, because he truly believes that they would despise him. He can't risk that happening – George and Annie are the only part of his life that is secure and which he absolutely cannot afford to lose. This is a vampire with emotions and feelings, a vampire who cannot accept himself or believe himself worthy of care and affection, but is doomed to live with those feelings forever. What Mitchell desperately wants to 'be', is human. When told by Herrick that it's time to decide whose side he's on (in the battle between vampires and humans), Mitchell replies 'I choose them'. But he can never be the same as them and that's his tragedy – he's neither fish nor fowl, man nor (entirely) beast.

This contradiction is illustrated when, in the present day, Mitchell recognises a patient in the hospital where he works as Josie, a woman who, had things gone to plan, should have been one of his victims forty years earlier. Yet we learn via flashbacks that Mitchell actually fell in love with Josie – and rather than killing her, the pair found themselves in an almost human relationship. Somehow, a bloodthirsty vampire managed to have an intimate relationship with a human woman without killing her, showing that he could control his bloodlust in certain cases – that there was still a glimmer of humanity within the bloodthirsty vampire. There's no suggestion that Mitchell ceased killing, just that he chose not to kill this particular person. With Josie, he wasn't solely an animal, functioning purely on instinct. He was, deep down, human.

Adam and Eve, the main characters in Jim Jarmusch's gorgeous 2013 movie *Only Lovers Left Alive,* live not in Eden, but thousands of miles apart on different continents – one in Tangiers, Morocco, the other in Detroit, Michigan. Lovers for centuries, the ennui radiates off them. Tom Hiddleston's Adam in particular is troubled – and dangerously so. But the risk's towards himself, rather than those around him. A famous musician who over the centuries has inspired many of the biggest names in music, Adam is terrified of being discovered. Having existed for so long that he no longer sees anything interesting in the world, Adam prefers to languish dramatically, the epitome of the glamorously doomed rock star. He lives a hermit-like existence, the desire to further his music quashed by his fear of discovery, and is reduced to visiting a hospital contact in the middle of the night to get the blood he craves (the pair stopped feeding indiscriminately years earlier, fearing contamination from the blood supply of those living in the modern world).

On the other side of the world, Tilda Swinton's Eve gets her own supplies from the couple's old friend Christopher Marlowe, played by John Hurt (we later discover that, in this timeline at least, the literary theories are true – Marlowe did indeed write most of Shakespeare's plays). The connection between Adam and Eve has developed such a depth over the centuries that she can sense his distress even across great distances and she travels (rather reluctantly) to Detroit in order to help him. Their reunion is disrupted by the arrival of Eve's younger sister Ava from Los Angeles. Ava finds the older couple boring and does her level best to shake up their entire lives as casually as she might shake a snow globe. Even as they attempt to curb the girl's wayward appetites one can see that the unaccustomed excitement is finally breaking through the shell of safe isolation that Adam and Eve have constructed around themselves.

In the manner of irritating younger siblings since time immemorial, Ava drinks all the 'good stuff' in the house and drags the unwilling pair out to a nightclub, where Adam is disconcerted to hear his own music being played by the live band. Waking up the next evening, Eve discovers that Ava has killed Adam's acolyte, Ian, leading to the kind of conversation that might be expected between any parent of an errant teenage daughter. A groggy Ava is shaken awake to explain what she's done, 'Ohhhh I didn't mean to, he was just so cute and now I feel sick.' Eve rolls her eyes so much that it's a wonder they don't fall out and roll down the hall, 'Well what did you expect? He's from the fucking music industry!' Which just goes to show that teenagers – and musicians – are the same the world over, regardless of their immortal status.

Having kicked Ava out of the house and disposed of Ian's body in an acid bath, the pair are further disturbed by the arrival outside the house of some of Adam's fans and escape back to Tangier with only the belongings they can carry, only to discover that Marlowe has unwittingly drunk contaminated blood in their absence and is dying.

The vampires' glacier-slow, dreamlike existence gives an otherworldly air to a movie that is in no rush to do anything other than blind the viewer with its sheer ethereal beauty. In Adam and Eve's universe, everything can wait – they have all the time in the world.

Immortality can sometimes be too much to bear for even the most hardened of bloodsuckers. The 'death by contaminated blood' trope used in *Only Lovers Left Alive* is one which reappears in the 2020 television adaptation of *Dracula*. We first become aware of the Count's deadly kryptonite when he attempts to drink from Zoe Van Helsing. Unbeknownst to him, Zoe has cancer – as soon as he swallows the first mouthful of her blood, he is reduced to a retching animalistic heap on the floor, bloody-black vomit dripping from his mouth. Zoe uses this as a weapon towards the end of the adaptation, warning the newly undead Lucy Westenra that if she bites her, she will die a final, horrible death.

This 'blood as suicide' mirrors an earlier scene in *Dracula* that takes place on the *Demeter*. A young girl who is travelling on the ship with her father drinks poison rather than risk being turned into a vampire by her predatory fellow passenger. But in his own final moments, Dracula is not escaping a fate worse than death – rather, he is taking the final step into oblivion that he has subconsciously craved for so many centuries. When he drinks Zoe's blood, he takes her with him into a dream state within which she can escape the pain and loneliness of death. In reality she is lying fully clothed on a table, but in her death dream, Zoe is lying naked and entwined with her-long time adversary in their first and last truly intimate encounter.

What Zoe has discovered as she takes her last painful breaths is that Dracula is ashamed. Ashamed of not being able to die, while having to witness the deaths of all those around him (including his own mortal family), and ashamed of being scared to even face death at all. He has been forced to exist for centuries longer than he wanted to. He's developed a hatred of mirrors, not because they betray him to others, but because they show him his true self – an ancient, crumbling, walking corpse. Dracula is controlled by shame and societal constructs as much as anyone, his immortality doing nothing to save him either from the opinions of others or his own opinion of himself.

The final death is, to Dracula, a blessed escape, and he walks into it in the arms of the one person who has always been his equal. Dracula and Agatha/Zoe need each other, right up until their last (un)dying breaths. While also using the situation to his own advantage, the Count's last words are undoubtedly ones of kindness. 'After all this time, did you think I would let it hurt?'

The word 'vampire' is never once uttered in *The Hunger*, yet we all know exactly what's going on. The film opens with Catherine Deneuve and David Bowie stalking a nightclub like the glamorous predators they are soon shown to be. The band Bauhaus play *Bela Lugosi's Dead* on a huge screen, singer Peter Murphy looming ominously over the crowd. Probably the most recognisable of all goth anthems – and widely accepted as having been the first goth single to be released – the threatening monotone of the introduction tells you immediately what you can expect from the rest of the movie.

What could be more beautiful than David Bowie as a doomed vampire? This is the Starman himself, prowling for victims alongside his beautiful companion/mistress. Bowie was as celebrated for his acting as much as his music and, although the former might not always have been the most successful of his career sidelines, his lean physique and sculpted facial features lent themselves to playing otherworldly characters. In *The Hunger*, Bowie is John, an eighteenth-century cellist who is the perfect foil to the icily beautiful Miriam, Deneuve's manipulative elder vampire. As with all Miriam's previous victims, John has been promised eternal life at her side. The only prerequisite is that John has to occasionally feed on humans in order to stay 'alive'. And Miriam hasn't lied to John – he does indeed have the gift of eternal life. What he doesn't have is eternal *youth*. After 200 years of glamorous undeath, John suddenly begins to decay, ageing decades in a matter of days. Despite killing and feeding in a hopeless attempt to halt the process, nothing can stop his decline. In desperation, he attempts to seek the advice of leading gerontologist Sarah Roberts, but is rebuffed. He begs Miriam to kill him in order that he might be released, but she ignores his pleas. Instead, she calmly places him in one of many coffins in the attic, all of which contain Miriam's previous lovers. We hear their cries for true death even as she clicks briskly off in her neat heels, leaving her past lovers to their unending doom. John has been gifted eternal life in the most terrible way possible – with no existence other than eternal 'un-death'. He and his fellow discarded victims have no escape from being trapped in their decaying shells with full awareness of what's happening to them.

Having realised that something is indeed terribly wrong, Sarah returns to the apartment and is seduced by Miriam, who plans to install her as

John's replacement. The older woman is, however, eventually outplayed by Sarah, who forces Miriam to swallow her blood in a reversal of the expected roles. Miriam is then attacked by her own victims who have begun to rise from their tombs – as she falls to her doom, she ages all those missing, static centuries as she hits the floor.

In the final scenes of *The Hunger*, a large draped box – conveniently coffin-sized – lies behind a mesh screen, echoing Murphy's opening appearance in the movie. As we watch Sarah gazing out over the city from her balcony, a voice screams her name from inside the box. Miriam has finally met her own eternal fate.

*The Hunger*'s interpretation of vampirism portrays an 'alpha' character sacrificing others in order that they alone might 'live' on. The bloody baton is passed from one vampire to the next – Sarah already has a young female companion with her, even as Miriam's cries ring out unheard (or ignored) from her tomb.

Miriam Blaylock is as far from having morals as she is from being alive. After centuries of using humans for both company and sustenance, Miriam is more instinctive creature than human, simply moving onto the next food source as each of her victims is drained of the last of their life force. By the time that John realises the horror of his predicament, it is already too late – Miriam is ready to move on to her next victim. Miriam might weep along with John as she entombs him, but hers is a pragmatic sadness, just something that comes with the territory.

Criticised at the time of release for the perceived sluggishness of the storyline along with a very thin plot, *The Hunger* has nevertheless gained a cult following over the years, helped along by its deeply gothic overtones. Few could disagree that the film has more than its fair share of faults, yet its continued popularity illustrates just how much an audience loves a pale, languorous – and above all, beautiful – vampire.

# Chapter Five

# Virtue and Vampires

Is it possible for vampires to ever be considered moral? We are quick to condemn them as being the epitome of evil, which in many ways is understandable – after all, by definition they drain the blood and the life out of their (often innocent) victims. But is that any different to a living, mortal human killing and eating an animal? We tend to judge the vampire by our own morals without stopping to consider our own behaviour. Despite killing carelessly and freely, Count Dracula's tragic backstory in Francis Ford Coppola's *Bram Stoker's Dracula* makes it almost impossible to see him as *entirely* evil. Powered by love and loss, the Count strides a murderous path through Victorian England, and is all the more attractive for it. We might not understand murder, but most of us can understand lust – and this Dracula is the embodiment of animalistic, lustful urges.

Modern vampires might sparkle and prefer eating animals to munching on humans, but even their 'vegetarian' diet doesn't prevent them breaking moral taboos when it suits them. So do we simply like vampires so much because they refuse to stick to society's rules? Are they so tempting precisely *because* they're not held to the societal expectation which itself keeps modern society from simply running amok? Or perhaps we envy their ability to set their own moral boundaries, rather than being constrained by those held by human society.

According to some traditions, rather than being banished by God for being insubordinate, Lilith – Adam's first wife in the Garden of Eden – in fact left of her own accord in order to become queen of the demons, preying on the blood of babies. Presumably this was a more acceptable reason than a woman simply knowing her own mind. Society has long placed strictures on what is 'acceptable' human behaviour. The oldest stories in existence are invariably morality tales, illustrating what happens to those who fail to adhere to the boundaries placed upon them by others. Anyone stepping outside the lines is punished, often severely. Sex is power. And the withholding of sexual favours is the only way to keep hold of some of that power for ourselves – or at least, that's what we're told.

Many in the nineteenth century believed that the human body was a 'closed system' and that the loss of any bodily fluids risked weakening a person, potentially terminally. Given, then, that vampire stories invariably involve both loss of blood through being bitten and bodily fluids from sexual activity, is it any wonder that lustful, undead bloodsuckers delivered such a frisson of excitement to readers who were otherwise restricted in their personal lives? This 'vampire as morality tale' angle struck such a chord that it has barely crept back into the coffin over the intervening years. Even the most prim of readers can indulge themselves in tales of dark forces and deadly lust while telling themselves that they would never give in to temptation, if they were in the same situation. Purity is power, is what the stories tell us, and if we are pure we will be rewarded in some way – even if that 'reward' is simply arriving in the afterlife rather sooner than expected.

In most vampire stories, it is women who are expected to live up to the moral standards set by others. As far back as *The Vampyre*, Polidori tells of women being seduced by his protagonist and inevitably dying as a consequence. In the *True Blood* series, Maudette Pickens is a tragic young woman who, it is implied, has become promiscuous in order to assuage her loneliness. Or perhaps her loneliness stems from the promiscuity, which has clearly cheapened her in the eyes of those who know her. Maudette's murder is all but seen as an inevitable consequence of her behaviour – sexual confidence once again becoming a by-word for 'less valuable'. Those who die at the hands of vampires – or as collateral damage around them – are responsible for their own fate, we are told, because they were not strong enough to resist their animalistic urges.

Mina and Lucy are individuals both in Stoker's original story and in many of the endless adaptations. But in effect they are two sides of the same human coin – the woman as Madonna/whore, as eternal a trope as ever existed. Jonathan Harker might be the naive man who has to learn to literally fight for his life in order to save his woman, but his is a basic character, despite his constant presence in the story – Harker is a pawn who is used for the furthering of both the Count's journey and our own literary adventure. One could argue that Jonathan Harker is, in fact, perhaps the least important of any of the characters in *Dracula*.

Lucy Westenra met a miserable fate through Stoker's pen for the crime of being a sexually awakened young woman. Loved by everyone she meets – both male and female – and openly desired by men, Lucy is clear about her emotions and desires in a way that was definitely not considered acceptable in nineteenth-century society. Unable to decide between her many suitors, Lucy expresses her desire to have *all* of them, in order that everyone concerned might get what they desire and lead happier lives as a result. In Coppola's film adaption, especially, she is easy pickings for the newly arrived Count, who sees nothing wrong in brainwashing, seducing and killing the oldest and dearest friend of his ultimate target. Lucy is merely a stepping stone on his journey towards his end goal – to have Mina for himself. Dracula toys with Lucy much as a cat would with a mouse that it has brought in from the garden, deciding whether it can be bothered to kill. He haunts her in both mind and body, condemning her to a slow and torturous death while using her to sate both his hunger and his lust.

By the time Dracula was published, Bram Stoker was a thoroughly upright member of society. One has to wonder how much of his own hidden desires were subsumed into the Count's amoral behaviour, and whether he was considering how freeing it would be to drop the social mores and just plough through life without a care for others, following only his own desires. Despite being restricted to sleeping in coffins and occasionally living quite literally like an animal, Count Dracula is a free spirit in a way that was all but impossible for those in Victorian society. It can be no coincidence that the thirst for vampire stories began in earnest in the nineteenth century. The era of Queen Victoria and starched collars, prim manners and social rules that spread across continents, the 1800s were, on the surface at least, a carefully supervised epoch of industrial progress and human endeavour. But underneath the god-fearing heart of the Victorian epoch lay a seething, boiling mass of fear, loathing and lust. Society was changing rapidly and industrial advancements were altering landscapes all over the world.

Sexuality may have been hidden underneath complex layers of societal politeness and careful manners in the nineteenth century, but humans are animals at heart. Our base instincts never truly disappear, they're just more carefully covered up. You can be sure that any licentious urges we take for granted in our current, more broadminded, age weren't invented in 1963, whatever Philip Larkin liked to say. Dark fantasies have existed since humans had time for imagination and have been lurking just under the surface ever since.

At the time Polidori wrote *The Vampyre*, society was in a period of massive change across the world. Victoria would soon come to the throne – the first 'modern' British monarch, with a healthy libido and no inclination to hide her desire for her beloved consort, Prince Albert. The British Empire was about to hit its peak, with outposts springing up across Africa, the Middle East and Asia. Change was happening on a massive scale across the globe. Travel to other continents was becoming increasingly possible for more people and with it came awareness of other cultures and attitudes. In America, European immigrants were claiming land in a greedy swarm, overwhelming those who were native to the continent and revving up the racially aggravated war machine.

The first Industrial Revolution had given us electricity and the second was gearing up to change industry – and with it, our way of life – forever. The printing press brought newspapers carrying stories of gossip and scandal, along with paperback 'pulp' novels which found a willing readership in those looking for something to while away the time while travelling on the new rail services. In 1858 the diary of Isabella Robinson, telling of her romantic liaisons with a male friend, was used against her in court by her husband seeking a divorce. His plea was denied on the basis that no decent woman would allow herself to get involved in such things – his wife's lovelorn missives were deemed a work of fiction and thus inadmissible. The novel *East Lynne* by Ellen Wood (writing as Mrs Henry Wood, in the patriarchal style of the time) told a dramatic tale of a woman whose desire for another man brought about her inevitable downfall (including witnessing the death of her own child while being unable to confess to being his mother, Victorian fiction not being restrained when it came to pathos).

Sex was severely restricted on a moral and social level, with young men and women being taught that it was a force for evil and could only be safely channelled through heterosexual married relationships, and then preferably only for the begetting of children. Masturbation was an unspoken horror with countless remedial devices on offer. Grim illustrations were published in popular journals, showing in graphic detail how quickly 'self love' could destroy one's health and happiness (it usually involved lying around on chaises looking pallid and pox-ridden).

Desire killed – at least, according to those who would wish to set boundaries on others.

The twentieth century dawned more promisingly, at least for those of a libertarian nature. Queen Victoria died in 1901 after her record-breaking tenure on the throne and was replaced by her son, the notoriously louche Prince of Wales. The newly minted King Edward, already no stranger to scandal, went as far as to invite several of his favourite ladies to his coronation, including court favourite Alice Keppel, great-grandmother to Camilla Parker Bowles, wife of the current Prince of Wales. The women were seated in a roped-off section referred to by other guests in the know as 'the royal loose box'.

But darkness was looming on the Continent and the Great War brought with it more misery and loss than anyone could have predicted back in those heady days of the Empire and its never-setting sun. No wonder, then, that the people took solace in imaginary worlds.

The advent of commercial cinematography brought stories to life, quite literally in front of the viewer's eyes. The earliest screen vampire certainly wasn't imbued with the sensual glamour we have come to expect. German film director F.W. Murnau might been refused permission to adapt *Dracula*, but he wasn't going to be stymied by something as minor as legalities. *Nosferatu: A Symphony of Horror* was an almost literal reworking of Stoker's story, with just the names and some minor details changed. Max Schreck made an ugly and terrifying monster; one who perhaps looked more realistically like someone who had recently risen from the grave, but definitely lacking in sex appeal.

As the century wore on – and with it, more death and destruction, interspersed with periods of calm, when most people tried to forget about the outside world altogether – film makers began to make their vampires more appealing to an increasingly discerning audience. Despite the many adaptations and offshoots of the most famous fanged hero of our times, for many vampire aficionados, there can be only one Count Dracula.

Christopher Lee became all but the template for a noble, yearning Count in a series of Hammer Horror productions that taught us to take our vampires dark and delicious. Lee's Dracula is one who clearly sees himself as being above mere mortals on a social level, as well as an esoteric one. His clipped, public school tones mark him out as being socially superior to the poor country folk he invariably terrorises. Anyone who disturbs his murderous rampages is merely collateral damage, impolite enough to get in his way and deserving of their inevitably awful fate. The women he attacks are nothing more than lunch wrapped up in a pretty frock – silly little girls who should be grateful for his terminal intentions, portrayed as getting only what they deserve.

Hammer Film's *Dracula* (1958 – retitled *Horror of Dracula* in the United States, to avoid potential confusion with the 1931 Bela Lugosi version) would become the benchmark for celluloid vampires the world over, with Lee's looming presence the epitome of Bram Stoker's creation. Often acclaimed as one of the greatest horror movies of all time, *Dracula* changed public perception of the bloody thirsty Count. Lee's performance pushed the possibility that maybe, just maybe, some women might actively enjoy being chomped on by a vampire, as long as the vamp in question was tall, dark and deadly handsome (Christopher Lee was well aware of this and would later poke fun at his reputation by titling his autobiography *Tall, Dark and Gruesome*). Rather than hamming it up as Lugosi had done, or playing the monstrous awfulness to the hilt *a la* Max Schreck in *Nosferatu*, Lee played his Dracula completely straight. This was a Count who took his evil *seriously*. Many of the actors who played his victims have gone on record as saying just how enthusiastically Lee inhabited the role, becoming a genuinely terrifying presence on set. *Dracula* was filmed in Technicolour rather than black and white, which allowed director Terence Fisher to make full use of bloody special effects. A scene in which Dracula rips off his own skin – created by applying a layer of mortician's wax to Lee's face over the top of red makeup – was cut from the film for the domestic markets, but restored in 2012 from a rescued Japanese reel of the original film (the fully restored version is now widely available).

The first Hammer adaptation of the Dracula story to have a contemporary setting was *Dracula A.D. 1972* (which unsurprisingly came out in 1972), again starring Christopher Lee. Despite being hobbled by its clunky script, *A.D. 1972* has become something of a cult film over the intervening years precisely because of its lack of polish (bonus points for anyone who spotted the brief reference to it in the last episode of the 2020 BBC television adaptation of *Dracula*).

With every new film, Lee's version of the Count got ever more distant from his glamorously gothic origins. Yet the audience was still there for his dark and brooding vampire, nearly thirty years after he made his first appearance in the cloak – but why? There was a sense of 'otherness' about Christopher Lee, an air of being slightly above and apart from those around him. Some of this clearly comes from a place of privilege – Lee had the background and contacts that many aspiring actors would have killed for at the time, not to mention the kind of looks and voice that were perfect for a grimly sensual leading man. Luck of the biological draw, then, to some extent. But Lee also brought a personal touch to Count Dracula, taking the character absolutely seriously, even when he was being played for laughs. You can treat the story as a joke, Lee seemed to imply, but Dracula – well, he's something else entirely. Something that watches while the world changes around him, patiently waiting for common sense to return and for people to realise that he's still there – watching, waiting, sharpening his fangs.

*Byzantium* (2012) was another vampire movie from director Neil Jordan. Having found such success with *Interview With The Vampire* in 1994, Jordan would have been excused for thinking he'd done enough for the vampire cause already. The scope for critical failure was huge – how could a movie set in present-day Britain compete with the glossy vampires of Jordan's *Interview* adaptation? To further differentiate *Byzantium* from the usual vampire crowd, the main action takes place in a bleak and rundown boarding house in Hastings, on the south coast of England. Yet, somehow, *Byzantium* works. Elder vampire Clara's blowsy sexuality pushes the younger Eleanor's quiet confusion into sharp contrast and brings humanity to both characters in the process. Anyone who's visited a British seaside town in the off-season can imagine just how otherworldly it might be behind the cold and empty fronts of the promenade hotels. Based on a play by Moira Buffini, *Byzantium* pulls in historical and supernatural references with ease, drawing them into the present day with a casual and natural realism. Polidori's *The Vampyre* is referenced with the character of Captain Ruthven, as is Byron's *A Fragment...* by the inclusion of Midshipman Darvell.

Clara initially appears to be a rather unsympathetic character, dragging Eleanor with her as she lurches from one crisis to another. But we soon realise that the women's relationship is not what it initially appears and that Clara has good reason for her aggressively protective attitude. At its heart is a portrayal of the eternal fight against patriarchal power, a fight which – in this instance at least, and possibly only temporarily – is won by the matriarchs.

The idea of the virtuous vampire rose to a rather depressing pinnacle in Stephanie Meyer's *The Twilight Saga*, which rather heavy-handedly depicts 'good' versus 'bad'. In the world of *Twilight*, the sign of a good vampire apparently involves refusing to have sex before marriage and preferring lunch to have four legs rather than two. There is no disguising the influence of religion in this interpretation of the eternal love story. Edward Cullen – that perfect specimen of undead manhood who actually *sparkles* – is firm in his conviction that he has no soul and that he, along with all other vampires, is going straight to hell. How one actually gets to hell when one has no soul and is already dead is never explained, but Edward believes it anyway.

When Edward first takes Bella to meet his undead family, he notices her surprised expression when she sees that he and his family live in a bright and spacious modern house, rather than something more … traditional. 'What did you expect,' he asks her in amusement, 'coffins and dungeons and moats?' Well of course that's what she was expecting, because it's what we're used to seeing. Vampires are supposed to live in creepy, half-ruined desolation, not in multi-million-dollar houses filled with modern designer furniture and floor to ceiling windows. The vampires of Forks are sanitised for public consumption, their huge bank accounts and tasteful clothes smoothing their passage through the human world. Which is, in some ways, a clever approach on the creator's part – of *course* modern vampires need both money and luxury, because they are precisely the things which make it easier to hide in plain sight. But it also makes the Cullens *safe*. Even when Edward is telling Bella he might kill her, we kind of already know that he won't. Edward has too much of a conscience for a vampire – if he killed her he would invariably spend the rest of eternity tormenting himself with the ensuing guilt.

Carlisle Cullen is presented as the wise elder of the family; the patriarch who can be relied upon to make sure everyone is kept safe. Which of course he should, because it was Carlisle who created the family in the first place. Much is made of Carlisle's selflessness – it was he who discovered that it was possible to survive off animal blood, when he killed deer in desperation shortly after his own transformation. But in 1918 a lonely Carlisle, now a doctor, was working at a hospital dealing with victims of Spanish influenza, when one of his dying patients asked him to save her son Edward. Carlisle 'turned' Edward, telling himself he was fulfilling his promise while also gaining a companion. Three years later he did the same for Esme, when she was brought to the hospital after a failed suicide attempt. Clearly on a roll, Carlisle later also 'saved' Rosalie, who had been left for dead after being gang-raped by her fiancé and his friends (the *Twilight* saga is a strange beast in the way that it glosses over much unsavoury-ness only to hit the reader/viewer smack in the face with such unexpected horrors as an implied rape scene or, much later in the series, young girls having their heads ripped off even as those around her beg for mercy).

Did Carlisle really 'save' the first three members of his family? When one considers how much angst Edward has clearly been through about the ethics of his own existence, one could argue that it would have been kinder to let him die. Should any doctor – even a fictional one – ever make life or (un)death decisions on behalf of a patient who isn't in a fit state to give informed consent? What if those decisions are being made for the doctor's benefit? It's all well and good the story showing how Esme eventually fell in love with Carlisle, but I'm pretty sure that most people would *feel* as though they were (maybe) in love with someone who'd saved them from death, through sheer gratitude if nothing else. There's also the story of how Rosalie found love with Emmet – the fact that she rescued him after a bear attack is kind of romantic, but it becomes rather less so when we realise that she then carried him back to the Cullen residence (okay so it was apparently a journey of around 100 miles, which gives Rosalie bonus points for dedication). Yup, ol' Canine Cullen at your service – once again, Carlisle comes to the 'rescue', turning Emmet in order that he might live on as an eternal companion for Rose.

There is clearly an argument to be made that Carlisle has, in fact, acted in an incredibly selfish manner. He has technically murdered four people, regardless of the fact that they'd all have otherwise died. And he has taken the option of death away from them *forever*. His actions have forced all of eternity on four people who might actually have preferred not to have it (and Edward makes it pretty clear that he's felt like that at some points of his existence).

On paper, Edward is the Most Unsuitable Boyfriend Ever. But the storyline repeatedly insists that he is perfect, despite being murderous, dead and unable to go outside when the sun is shining. The 'sparkling in sunlight' trope was, in fact, conveniently ignored at points in the movie adaptations – in the first film of the series, director Catherine

Hardwicke had Robert Pattinson wear sunglasses in one scene, because the weather had turned brighter than expected and she didn't have the budget to wait for an overcast day. No one seems to notice Edward's sparkling skin, despite him having explained on many occasions that he and his family often hid away in case people saw them in the sun. The most important thing in *Twilight's* world of shiny vampiric misogyny is that Edward knows what's best for Bella. Even when she disagrees with him, he has no compunction in overriding her will in order to 'keep her safe'. The fact that Edward's idea of keeping his human safe equates to preventing them doing pretty much anything of their own free will appears to be neither here nor there. As far as Edward is concerned, Bella is nothing more than a silly, fractious human being and as such clearly cannot know her own mind. Enter Edward stage right, willing to manfully subdue his constant urge to rip out her throat in order to show her how to live her life better than she could manage on her own. Such noble sacrifice.

Within the first book alone, Edward tells Bella that she's imagining things (spoiler, she absolutely isn't) and that he wants to kill her but is trying his best not to (she seems to find this rather sweet, another side effect of being in close proximity to vampires presumably being that one loses all sense of self preservation). Oh, and she discovers that he is actually more than a century old. Rather than running away screaming like any sane person would, Isabella Swan takes all this in her stride. As far as Bella is concerned, being stalked by a man old enough to be her great-great-grandfather – and who would quite like to kill and eat her, don't forget – is actually the most romantic thing that could ever happen to a teenage girl.

The second book in the series, *New Moon*, has, as its starting point, Edward leading Bella deep into the woods in the dark of night, informing her that he's dumping her … and then running away and leaving her there alone. He disappears abroad after this major act of negligence, moping in dramatically photogenic fashion at various glamorous tourist destinations. His behaviour leaves Bella comatose, quite literally – the next four months of this teenage drama queen's life is depicted in the book as a series of blank pages. Our 'heroine' only regains her faculties when she hears that her lost love is determined to kill himself – at which point she risks everything to save him, including telling him that he's more worthy than she is. *New Moon* is almost entirely devoted to wherewithal women were wont to make their children afraid, according to these verses of *Lucilius*.

> *Terricolas Lamias, Fauni quas Pompiliq;*
> *Inflituere Numæ, tremit has, &c.*

Of these *Angelus Politianus* relateth this old wives story, in his preface upon *Aristotles* first book of Analyticks, that his Grand-mother told him when he was a childe, there were certain *Lamiæ* in the Wildernefs, which like Bug-bears would eat up crying boys, and that there was a little Well near to *Fefulanum*, being very bright, yet in continual fhadow, never feeing Sun, where these Phairy women have their habitation, which are to be feen of them which come thither for water.

A 1658 woodcut illustration of 'a lamia'. Lamia herself was a woman who allegedly took bloody vengeance after Hera destroyed her children. (Wellcome Collection. Attribution 4.0 International (CC BY 4.0))

Elisabeth Bathory – the vampiress who never was. (Public Domain)

An 1873 engraving of Lord Byron, artist unknown. Byron wrote the snippet of a story that inspired Polidori's later work and was himself the inspiration for Polidori's portrayal of the vampire as we know it today. (Public Domain)

Frontispiece from *The Vampyre* by
John William Polidori, 1819.
(Public Domain)

THE

VAMPYRE;

A Tale.

LONDON:

PRINTED FOR SHERWOOD, NEELY, AND JONES,

PATERNOSTER-ROW.

1819.

[Entered at Stationers' Hall, March 27, 1819.]

*Regina Cordium* by Dante
Gabriel Rossetti. Modelled by
his muse, Elizabeth 'Lizzie'
Siddal, her red hair would
come to haunt Rossetti (almost
literally) after her death from
a laudanum overdose in 1862.
(Public Domain)

Lizzie Siddal was buried in the Rossetti family vault in Highgate Cemetery, London, despite her husband's family having openly disapproved of her during her life. Dante Gabriel Rossetti left instruction that he himself should be buried elsewhere, presumably to avoid potential undead repercussions. (Violet Fenn)

Sheridan Le Fanu, author of *Carmilla*, the story of a sapphic vampire. Image from 1873 or earlier, photographer unknown. (Public Domain)

Bram Stoker, the godfather of modern vampire literature, c.1906. (Public Domain)

Whitby Abbey, forever associated with Bram Stoker's *Dracula*. (Tim Hill / Pixabay)

One of the two Victorian catacombs that still sit within Anfield Cemetery, Liverpool. After years of decay, the buildings are finally being rescued by the Friends of Anfield Cemetery. (Violet Fenn)

Legend has it that an undead Russian noblewoman lies in the vaults beneath the Anfield catacombs. (Violet Fenn)

Coffins were lowered into the Anfield catacombs via a mechanical pulley system. The 'trapdoor' through which they descended is now weighted down with old masonry. But is that to stop vandalism, or to prevent the residents escaping? (Violet Fenn)

Mortsafes at Kinnernie graveyard, Aberdeenshire. Often described as 'vampire graves', the iron cages were in fact installed to keep the deceased safe from would-be body snatchers. (Wellcome Collection. Attribution 4.0 International (CC BY 4.0))

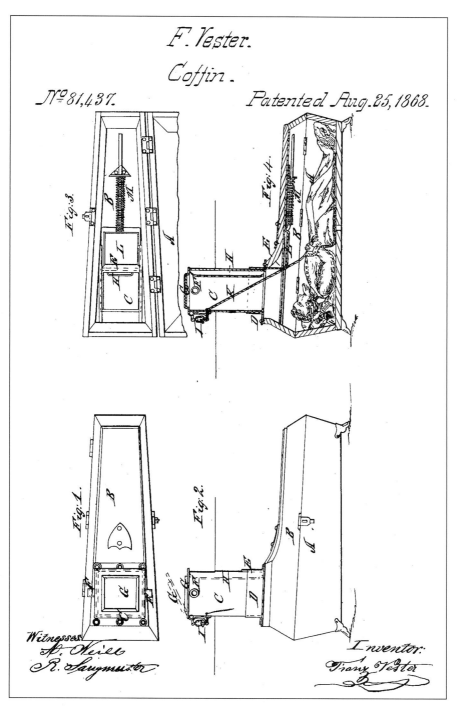

F. Vester's 'Improved burial case', 1868. The design included both a ladder and a bell, to facilitate escape if one was unfortunate enough to be buried prematurely. (United States Patent and Trademark Office)

*The Bite* – etching on paper, by Norwegian artist Edvard Munch (1914). (Public Domain CC0)

F.W. Murnau, director of *Nosferatu: A Symphony of Horror.* (Public Domain)

Max Schreck, aka *Nosferatu.*
(Public Domain)

Bela Lugosi - for many, the
perfect vampire archetype.
(Public Domain)

The gates to Glasgow Necropolis.
(Jacqueline Dooley Hamilton)

Glasgow Necropolis, the site of a mass vampire hunt by children in October 1954. Prompted by stories of the 'Gorbals Vampire', this display of public hysteria – stoked by newspaper reports – eventually led to the censorship of the then-popular 'horror comics'. (Jacqueline Dooley Hamilton)

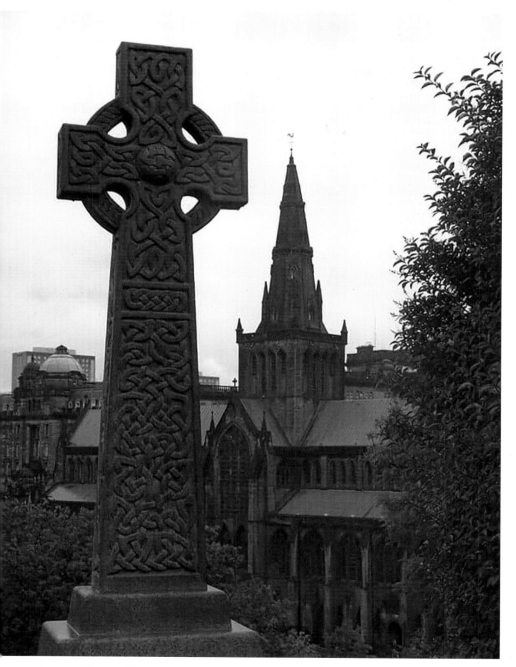

Glasgow Necropolis. (Laura Norkett Lui)

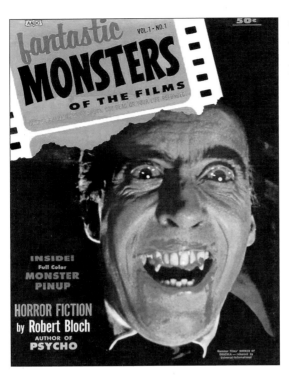

Christopher Lee on the cover of *Fantastic Monsters* horror comic, 1962. (Black Shield Publications Inc. / Public Domain)

William MacKenzies' unusual tomb in the graveyard of the former St Andrew's Church, Rodney Street, Liverpool. (Violet Fenn)

Highgate Cemetery, the location of a long-running feud between rival occultists, David Farrant and Sean Manchester. (Violet Fenn)

Coffins inside the catacombs of Highgate Cemetery. (Violet Fenn)

Dr Nadia Van Der Westhuizen.
(Steve Kenny)

Dr Nadia Van Der Westhuizen at Bran Castle, Romania. The castle is often described as the inspiration for Dracula's Transylvanian home, although it is up for debate as to whether Stoker even knew of its existence when he wrote his now legendary tale in 1897. (Dr Nadia Van Der Westhuizen)

showing how incomplete Bella is without Edward around to protect her, guide her, and tell her she's a klutz on a regular basis.

Thought it couldn't get any worse? Oh my sweet summer child, how wrong you are. In *Eclipse* – third in the series – Bella is used as the bait in an ambush that involves dozens of people risking their lives to fight for her right to party (with Edward). And – because this is the sort of thing that happens in Bella's world – she is sexually assaulted by Jacob, her supposed best friend. According to Jacob's logic, forcibly kissing someone against their will is a sign of eternal love and should be enough to convince them to leave their abusive partner for a life with you and your furry were-tongue. Again, all this weirdness is somehow seen by Bella as the sort of rightfully overwrought emotions that can only be expected when one truly loves an abusive, undead boyfriend.

Just to rub garlic into the emotional wounds of the previous books, the fourth and final episode of the saga, *Breaking Dawn,* is the longest of them all (long enough to require being divided into two movies for its cinematic adaptation). The length of the book appears to be entirely down to the focus on increasing the (by this point quite unreal) levels of coercion between various characters. Bella has grown old enough to decide she would quite like to have sex if you please, and – having had a cringingly awkward conversation with her father in the previous film, *Eclipse*, about the precise status of her virginity – Edward does the manful thing and agrees. But only if she marries him first, because apparently one can only deflower the love of one's life if she is bound to you both legally and financially beforehand. Presumably to make it harder for her to escape should she decide that, actually, an undead penis isn't as sexy as she thought it might be.

Of course, this being true love, Bella wakes up from her first ever night of passion covered in bruises, and then has to deal with her husband being angry with her for not being angry at him (honestly this sort of makes sense in the movie, but maybe we were all suffering from a mass outbreak of Stockholm syndrome at this point, having survived this far into the saga). Then she finds out she's pregnant, the baby tries to eat its way out, her wolfy best friend falls in love with the baby at first sight and vows to marry her when she's older (yes, that is as icky as it sounds) and drippy old Bella finally gets her wish and is turned into a vampire. One of the first things out of her mouth after her conversion is, 'I was born to be a vampire', which is both a dichotomy and also a really poor career choice. Her husband parades her around his family and friend like an undead trophy wife, she's been successfully isolated from the majority of her friends and family, and her baby, Renesmee, grows at such a rate of knots that her best friend is practically planning the wedding before poor old Nessy even hits school age. But hey – she got her man. Even if he *is* old enough to be Christopher Lee's dad.

According to most popular portrayals, becoming an immortal who has no option but to feed on humans apparently absolves us of guilt. It is a theory which makes sense, because eternal life would be rather miserable if it brought with it an endless case of existential angst. Whether on page or screen, vampires are commonly portrayed as having the inalienable desire (and absolute need) to use humans as a feed source if and when necessary. Yes, some vamps may abstain and congratulate themselves for doing so, but their moral code generally slips as soon as their alternate source of nutrition bites the silver bullet.

*Twilight* sets itself up to be morally 'good' from the start. The vampires of Forks choose not to drink human blood, and instead hunt animals as a 'vegetarian' alternative. Which makes them – in their own opinion, at least – morally superior to your standard, murderous vampires. Of course, they also suffer a suitable amount of guilt for being what they are, and use their supposedly ethical approach to justify their existence. In the twilight world of *Twilight*, the Cullens are the good guys in comparison to those vampires who feed off humans and are therefore somehow seen as less evolved, more parochial.

This argument would stack up better if it wasn't for the fact that the minute the Cullens have to call in vampire backup, for the final showdown in *Breaking Dawn*, the ethical rules are thrown out of the window. The family and friends that come to the Cullens' rescue are definitely not vegetarian, and they have no intentions of changing their diet simply to fit in with their hosts' house rules. Regardless of how well our sparkly heroes stick to their own restricted menu, their guests are allowed to chow down on the local populace with little more than a brief, 'Oh well, whatcha gonna do?' shrug of their glittery shoulders. Newly minted vamp Bella gets around this moral dilemma by simply not thinking about it too much, her human ethics having clearly gone out of the window along with the need for a toilet in her luxury bathroom.

*Dark Shadows* started out as what can only be described as a 'gothic soap opera', which ran on the ABC television network in the United States from

June 1966 until April 1971. The story of the wealthy Collins family and their complicated (and often supernatural) lives in Collinsport, Maine, *Dark Shadows* only began to really take off with the appearance of the vampiric Barnabas Collins (played by Jonathan Frid) several months into the first series. In the 2012 film version directed by Tim Burton (which follows more or less the same path as the original series, barring the occasional character/plot tweak), Johnny Depp is Barnabas, the vampire who has returned to Collinsport seeking vengeance. Condemned to everlasting torment in the 1700s by his spurned lover Angelique, a witch who, as revenge, killed his fiancée and then turned him into a vampire and had him buried 'alive', Collins has spent centuries plotting his revenge.

Barnabas is the ultimate family man, one who doesn't care what collateral damage he causes along the way, so long as his nearest and dearest are safe. While one cannot help but have some sympathy for Angelique – who was genuinely in love with Collins in her youth but carelessly discarded by him for the crime of being a mere servant – it cannot be denied that she perhaps bears a grudge a little too well. Played by Eva Green to gloriously evil perfection, the witch is now the epitome of the femme fatale, a walking depiction of lust in a business suit. What is interesting is the humanity of the issues the main characters face. Despite being undead creatures of the night, both Angelique and Barnabas are battling for what they believe to be right – he for the safety and security of his newly rediscovered family and she for the relationship to which she believes they are destined. The fact that they each see nothing wrong in destroying others along the way takes nothing away from the fact they are incredibly *human* in their desires. Even while they are physically fighting like, well, bat and banshee, the pair are clearly also refereeing a battle in their own heads about whether revenge or lust should win the day. But Barnabas Collins is, at heart, a family man – and as such, he must defeat the woman who is trying to destroy him with the power of her sexuality. His true love, of course, is the lip-nibblingly innocent Victoria, who is revealed to be a reincarnation of Collins's first love, Josette. Once again, the male character is the most powerful both morally and emotionally, invariably choosing the Madonna over the whore. It is rather satisfying to imagine Angelique and Lucy Westenra joining forces to found an undead chapter of the Pink Ladies from Grease, flicking their middle fingers to the patriarchy and swanning off into the moonlight in a swish of skirts and a cloud of musky scent.

When their old friend Christopher Marlowe dies in *Only Lovers Left Alive*, Adam and Eve lose their food supply along with their beloved friend. Marlowe was their source for the 'special supplies' which have enabled the couple to live a minimally murderous lifestyle for so long, and without him their currently lifestyle is doomed. On the brink of their final, true death, the pair stumble upon young lovers enjoying a romantic evening. Adam and Eve approach them in a friendly fashion, the last words spoken as they bare their fangs at their terrified lunch being, 'Well, what choice do we have?'

Despite their faintly wistful and empathic air, the couple still kill two young people with all their human lives ahead of them, simply because they're hungry. As vampires, they consider themselves to be superior to mere mortals and the occasional emergency snack is simply collateral damage. Adam and Eve feel no shame about who or what they are, and that gives them enormous power. Portrayals such as this are interesting in that the storyline shows no mitigating circumstances other than the need to survive. Adam and Eve don't waste time on moral concerns in the way the Cullens would – they're animals at heart and they will survive as such.

Viago Von Dorna Schmarten Scheden Heimburg (né von Blitzenburg) is a 379-year-old dandy who prides himself above all on having good manners. Viago might be an undead creature of the night but that's not going to stop him being polite about it, as he explains to the camera crew following his life and that of his 'flat mates' in the original film version of *What We Do In The Shadows*.

*What We Do In The Shadows* is a mockumentary about modern day vampires who share a house in a nondescript suburb of Wellington, New Zealand. Their confused moral code is presented as the normal day-to-day trials and tribulations of outsiders who are just quietly trying to get on with their lives. When Deacon (the youngster of the group at a mere 183 years old) tells the camera that he was once a Nazi vampire, during WWII – 'I don't know if you know that the Nazis lost that war?' – it's with a tone of wry bemusement, rather than any acknowledgement of the monster he was and still is.

There are endless snapshots of the undead friends having murderous fun across the centuries – hamming it up, raising a glass of blood to the camera and generally partying as though there's no tomorrow (which there won't have been for many of the humans they came into contact with). Petyr is the oldest vampire and also Deacon's 'sire' – a fact which is announced with great jollity. 'This *creature* flies at me … it dragged me back to this dark dungeon and bit into my neck … and just at the point of death this creature forced me to suck its foul blood. And then, it opened its wings like this,' Deacon gestures in the air, 'and hovered above me, screeching, *aaaaaaahhahaha! Now you are vampire!* And it was Petyr!' At this point the camera pulls back to reveal Petyr sitting next to Deacon like the surprise guest on a daytime show about family reunions. 'And we're still friends today.'

When the uptight Viago finds a new victim, he likes to 'show them a good time', as he explains brightly to camera, the expression of happy, boyish innocence completely at odds with his true nature. We watch from the shadows as a young woman sits on the sofa in the vampire house, talking excitedly of her plans for the future. Viago nods and smiles and encourages her, but at the same time is laying newspaper out on the floor in order to avoid getting blood stains on his upholstery. The woman lifts her feet to allow him to place the paper underneath her with no more than a momentary flicker of confusion. After all, what's threatening about newspaper? We can almost see her thought process – Viago might be a little bit odd, but he's also cute. And she is definitely going to let him kiss her at some point.

He lifts her hair carefully out of the way and she murmurs slightly, obviously expecting a bit of a nuzzle, only realising at the very last doomed second that she's actually about to become supper. When he accidentally rips her jugular and blood spurts everywhere in comedic, overblown awfulness, Viago is a picture of panic-stricken hunger *and* mortification, frantically trying to simultaneously both drink and prevent an embarrassing mess.

In a nod to the legend of Vlad the Impaler, Vladislav is an 862-year-old Romanian who is also known as 'The Poker'. Turned at 16 ('And that is why I always look sixteen! In those days, of course, life was tough for a sixteen year old'), Vladislav is the most 'old school' vampire of the group. Viago says of his friend, affectionately, 'He's a really great guy. A bit of a pervert. He has some pretty old ideas about things'.

As with any young man, Vladislav has relationship problems – it's just that his are to do with his arch nemesis, 'The Beast'. The 'Beast' turns out to be Vladislav's ex-girlfriend Pauline, who is the only person ever to have got the better of him in a fight. Expecting to be made guest of honour for the prestigious Unholy Masquerade (held in the Cathedral of Despair, which actually turns out to be the headquarters of a local bowling club), Vladislav is mortified when the privilege is instead bestowed upon Pauline. He takes to his coffin in a wailing, self-absorbed heap of teenage hormones, despite being almost nine centuries old. He and Pauline fight, they get back together, they fight again – like couples the world over have done since time immemorial.

Vladislav, Viago and Deacon are genuinely heartbroken when Petyr is killed by a vampire hunter. The hunter had been accidentally alerted to their presence in the city by Nick, the newest and least wanted member of the vampire family. Nick was himself 'turned' by Petyr and Deacon's jealous behaviour is akin to an older brother being forced to tolerate a younger sibling who has arrived without warning and is now taking up all of his parents' attention. The genius of *What We Do In The Shadows* is in its absolute humdrum normality. Regardless of the main characters all being undead, they live and argue and fret like everyone else, with hurt feelings and confused relationships aplenty. Their only real fun appears to come from goading the local werewolf pack – motto, 'We're werewolves, not swear-wolves' – like a group of bored teenagers picking fights with rival gangs.

A running backstory throughout *Shadows* is Viago's abiding love for his (human) ex-girlfriend Katherine, who is now 96 years old and living in supported accommodation. He often spends his evening watching through her windows, which is reminiscent of Edward's creep-tastic stalking behaviour in *Twilight*. At the end of the film we discover that Viago has confessed all to Katherine, who agrees to let him 'turn' her in order that they might finally be together forever. The fresh faced vampire and the elderly Katherine are unconcerned about the age gap, but not in the way you might expect.

| | |
|---|---|
| Viago: | 'Some people freak out a bit about the age difference. They think, "What's this 96-year-old lady doing with a guy four times her age?" And, you know, I don't care.' |
| Katherine: | 'It doesn't make any difference.' |
| Viago: | 'No. They can call me cradle snatcher, who cares?' |

The innocence with which the pair discuss their love for each other – glossing over the fact that he has had to kill her in order to keep her with him, and that murder is just a way of life – is light-hearted and joyful, with an innocence rarely found in the outside world (another example of turning dark and light in on themselves to brilliant effect can be found in Tim Burton's *Corpse Bride* – not discussed here because it's not a vampire movie, it is nevertheless a must-see for anyone who likes their romance dark and fantastical).

In contrast, Elizabeth 'Betsy' Taylor's morals are almost her undoing on many occasions. The hero of MaryJanice Davidson's 'Undead' series, Betsy's story starts when, in the first book *Undead and Unwed*, she gets hit by a car on her thirtieth birthday and wakes up dead. Betsy has been pissed off about it ever since, mostly because she didn't ask to be Queen of the Vampires – the title was thrust upon her before she knew what was happening. As were the attentions of her 'husband', Eric Sinclair (who she likes to call Sink-lair, just to wind him up). While undoubtedly traumatised by her inability to stay awake in the daytime or change her hairstyle (however much Betsy styles it, it has always returned to its original state when she wakes up the next evening), this is a portrayal of a modern woman who isn't going to let a minor detail such as being dead – and a vampire, to boot – get her down.

No coffins and secrecy for this babe – Betsy lives in a mansion with her two best friends and is open with her family about her newly undead state (some relatives cope with this news better than others). What Betsy hasn't quite managed during her transformation is to let go of her idealistic approach to other humans (or animals). When she discovers a group of feral vampires who have been abandoned by her arch-nemesis, she ignores pleas by those around her to destroy them and instead determines to reintegrate them into society. This involves teaching one of them to knit (and occasionally letting him drink from her wrist). The Fiends, as she affectionately calls them, pay her back by killing one of her closest friends, but Betsy still can't bring herself to blame them – after all, they're simply following their natural urges. She also doesn't like the idea of feeding from humans, so makes a point of trying to only attack those who somehow 'deserve' their fate. A one-woman vampire vigilante team, Betsy prowls dark alleyways on the lookout for would-be rapists and murderers – and she always does it in heels.

'There's worse things out here tonight than vampires.'
'Like what?'
'Like me.'

Eric Brooks, aka 'Blade'

Eric Brooks is a half-vampire vigilante, better known as Blade. Based on the Marvel Comics superhero, Blade is what is commonly known as a *dhampyr* – the hybrid child of a male vampire and female human. There are some stories that have the gender/species mix the other way around, but these are rare. This is possibly due to the oft-suggested belief that male vampires have a high sex drive, but it could also be because female vampires are commonly portrayed as being infertile or physically incapable of carrying a foetus to term, even if they are able to conceive.

Dhampyrs are also known as daywalkers for their ability to, well, walk around in the daylight. Mostly Slavic in origin, dhampyr are, according to legend, generally portrayed as having all of the strengths of a vampire, tempered with the useful bits of being human. They don't get burned by sunlight and they lack the killer thirst that makes their full-blood brethren such uncomfortable neighbours. Interestingly, dhampyrs sometimes hunt down other hybrids as well as full-blooded vampires, perhaps through resentment at not quite belonging to either social group.

Which is where Blade comes in. Eric Brooks was borne of a human mother and vampire father and has spent his life working as a vigilante, attempting to cleanse the world of as many vampires as possible (he also has a terrible haircut/moustache combo, but let's not dwell on that right now). When haematologist Dr Karen Jenson is attacked, he can't bring himself to leave her to either die or transform into vampire, so brings her back to the hideout he shares with his friend and mentor, Abraham Whistler. Whistler is a human whose wife and daughters were killed by vampires many years previously – he has since dedicated his life to finding ways of destroying the deadly undead.

*Blade* treads carefully across accepted vampire lore while still taking the opportunity to poke gentle fun at some of the more tired tropes. In Blade's world, vampires are themselves divided into a form of caste system, with the 'pure bloods' – those who were born as vampires – at the top of the heap. These control an underworld that includes a faction of younger vampires led by Deacon Frost, who were turned during their human lives and are therefore considered inferior. Frost doesn't hold with tradition and even goes out in sunlight, by the simple expedient of covering himself in high factor sun cream. He and his followers see themselves as the new wave of vampire society, determined to overthrow the old guard.

Garlic still wards off the bloodsuckers in the *Blade* series, but in this world it works by inducing anaphylactic shock. This is a characteristic Whistler puts to good use by using it in 'vampire mace' – a mixture of garlic and silver nitrate carried in a small spray canister. Sunlight is also weaponised in the form of a UV flashlight, handy for torturing those enemies who need some encouragement to spill their inside information. Sexual overtones are not subtle in *Blade*, which includes more than one scene showing Blade's mother reacting to him in an erotically charged manner. Of course, she was separated from him at the moment of birth, just as she changed into a vampire – so one could perhaps argue that the woman pressing seductively up against him is, in essence, a completely different person. But one can't avoid the uncomfortable Oedipal overtones of their physical closeness, which is reinforced when Blade kills his mother for being, quite literally, a monster.

*Blade* is a far from perfect movie – there are endless bloopers if you know where to look (IMDb is your friend here). Both the acting and scene-setting are cheesier than a pound of Cheddar, even taking into account its comic book origins. It's impossible not to smirk just a tiny bit as Wesley Snipes delivers such gems as 'Some motherfuckers have always got to ice skate uphill,' with a deadly serious look on his face. But as a new take on an old idea, it's hard to beat.

Sometimes a film becomes notorious primarily for the sheer levels of technicolour psychopathy – and it's not always the vampires that are the clear-cut bad guys. *From Dusk Till Dawn* (1996) was Quentin Tarantino's first paid scriptwriting assignment and one in which he also starred, alongside George Clooney. The story of gleefully criminal brothers Seth and Richie Gecko, it starts as a bloodbath and gets gorier from there on in. When the brothers are inadvertently caught up in a den of vampires, along with the family they've kidnapped and forced to act as their drivers, the film turns into a never-ending rollercoaster of blood, fangs and even more violence than before. The joy of *From Dusk Till Dawn* is in its blatant and unashamed lack of morals on the part of pretty much everyone involved.

As with most fictional subjects, we can often find comfort in channelling our own world view through the all-powerful vampires we see portrayed in popular culture. Cinema audiences have for decades scared themselves silly imagining that the prowling vampire on the big screen is looking for them personally and teenage girls in their millions gave a lot of thought about how they'd look as a member of the bloodthirsty undead when *Twilight* hit the mainstream. Some people take their fascination with vampire morality that one step further.

'I guess it's a kind of vampire therapy.' Fran Hansen is a hair and makeup artist from Shrewsbury. We're sitting in the living room of her cosy, eccentric home, playing the computer game The Sims while being closely supervised by her elderly cat, Mowzer. I'm here for the vampires. I'd long known about Fran's obsession with her Sims characters. She regularly posts updates on social media and I – along with many others – have become rather over-invested in the wellbeing of the imaginary 'people' who live inside her computer. My fascination grew exponentially when she developed vampire characters, because most of Fran's vampires are different – they're vegan.

Diagnosed with bipolar affective disorder and always open about her ongoing mental health issues, Fran uses her Sims to help her make sense of the world around her, telling me that when she was younger, she used to run her Sims through different social situations to see how they responded and to 'practice' coping with such events herself. Through her laptop, she can develop 'her' vampire characters, turning them from murderous monsters to caring and upstanding members of an invisible society. One family even runs its own 'vegan veterinary surgery' – although its clients are limited as, being owned by vampires, it's only open after dark.

This might be a computer simulation game, but Fran's vampires have personal issues recognisable to many humans, even if they don't admit it publicly. Elven and Strom are sisters, based on the Grady twins from *The Shining*. They have mother issues – and who wouldn't, if they'd spent their babyhood being hissed at by someone who was supposed to care for them? But familial traumas aside, Fran's Sims aren't allowed to suffer unnecessary trauma – no third party add-ons containing murder and mayhem for this digital family.

'There's too much reality in reality. I don't want my Sims to have horrible things happen to them. I want them to have a happy nice life.'

**You want a happy nice life for characters that most people would see as the bad guys?**
'Yeah.'

**So you're starting with people who are the bad guys and you're trying to make them the good bad guys.**
'Frankenstein's monster – he gets chased, you know? But it's not his fault. I remember watching old films and feeling really sorry for the monsters. They don't always want to be monsters. They can't help how they are. No one asks to be a monster, do they? Monsters are created – I'm not talking about murderers or psychopaths, but people … sometimes bad things happen to them. Vampires didn't ask to be vampires, they were changed [against their will]'

**It's that thing of having sympathy with the monster, isn't it?**
'It's about being misunderstood – people judging you before they know you. Why do we even have those assumptions? The [Sims] game forces you to make moral decisions and you see the consequences.'

**So what's your plan for 'your' vampires?**
'I've always been tempted to write in one of them having an affair, but I don't think I can do it! I don't know why.'

One of the vampires even steals a neighbour's cat, because he believes he can look after it better. These vamps really do have morals – and they stick to them better than most humans.

# Chapter Six

# Dead Sexy

There is nothing quite so safe as a sexual fantasy written on the page. We have indulged ourselves in wonderfully unlikely stories since time immemorial, safe in the knowledge that while we might never dare to actually enact the things we read, somewhere deep in our psyche an imaginary version of us is living the immoral high life with no fear of the reprisals we might suffer in the real world. We get a frisson of excitement from sitting on public transport reading about characters we desire or admire getting up to all manner of transgressions, our fellow passengers oblivious to any erotic impropriety going on in our heads. Fantasy transcends guilt – and vampires transcend their own potential guilt by using 'glamour' to force their victims into actively desiring their fate. A form of mind control, glamouring a victim makes them believe that they are offering themselves willingly, while also allowing them to be suitably horrified after the fact. 'But he made me do it!' could possibly be seen as a very convenient way of avoiding censure for one's behaviour.

Legends of incubus and succubus are an example of 'demons' stealing life-force through sexual connection rather than drinking blood, yet the effects are the same – the draining of health by an unseen and unwanted force. This version of the life-sucking predator is almost always portrayed as being rather enjoyable for the 'victim', such creatures having developed rather more attractive looks over the course of the centuries. In a similar manner to the more modern vampires, there are endless folk tales of women who have been molested against their will by a night-time visitor. Tales of the incubus go back as far as 2400 BC and the Summerian King List, in which the father of Mesopotamian king, Gilgamesh, is listed as 'lilu'. A *lilu* was a faceless demon which preyed on women by attacking them through their dreams and defiling them while they slept. The female equivalent – the *lilitu* – were 'sex-crazed demons' which bear great similarity to the biblical story of Lilith. Supposedly laying upon sleeping men in order to sate their own desires, the lilitu would steal the men's purity and drain them of their physical strength.

In 1597, several years before the publication of his authorised version of the Bible, King James VI of Scotland (later to also become James I of England) wrote a dissertation titled *Daemonologie, In Forme of a Dialogue, Divided into three Books: By the High and Mighty Prince, James &c.* Written as a dialogue between the characters Philomathes and Epistemon, James works through the logistics required for such creatures to impregnate a human woman.

> By two meanes this great kinde of abuse might possibly be performed: The one, when the Deuill onelie as a spirite, and stealing out the sperme of a dead bodie, abuses them that way, they not graithlie seeing anie shape or feeling anie thing, but that which he so conuayes in that part […] The other meane is when he borrowes a dead bodie and so visiblie, and as it seemes vnto them naturallie as a man converses with them. But it is to be noted, that in whatsoeuer way he vseth it, that sperme seemes intollerably cold to the person abused. For if he steale out the nature of a quick person, it cannot be so quicklie carryed, but it will both tine the strength and heate by the way, which it could neuer haue had for lacke of agitation, which in the time of procreation is the procurer & wakener vp of these two natural qualities. And if he occupying the dead bodie as his lodging expell the same out thereof in the dewe time, it must likewise be colde by the participation with the qualities of the dead bodie whereout of it comes.

> *The Thirde Booke of Daemonologie,*
> King James VI, 1597

In short, James has worked out that, should a demon steal the sperm of a living man in order to use it for the impregnation of a human woman, the vital liquid would be cold and all but useless by the time it has been transported between donor and recipient. Therefore, the incubus must, in fact, be both male and female at the same time, able to transform between biological sex in order to be able to take sperm from a human male (as the female recipient) and then transfer it to a human female (as the male donor).

Incubi are relevant to vampire theory because many people believed demons to be capable of taking possession of a corpse and using it for their own 'costume', in order to walk the earth as the undead while appearing to be human. The myths were, even back in the sixteenth century, already beginning to separate revenants from what we would now know as vampires. But the idea of the undead walking the earth and using their supernatural abilities to seduce humans was beginning to settle into the foundations of the myths we know and love today.

Incubus and succubus have appeared in differing forms throughout history, humans always liking a scapegoat for both their moral and physical ailments, and they exist in varying forms across continents and cultures.

The lidérc is a Hungarian demon which can present itself in the guise of a lost loved one to a lonely woman. Seducing its victim on a nightly basis over some length of time, the lidérc gradually drains her blood, leaving her to waste away (the lidérc can also present itself as a *csodacsirke*, the rather brilliantly named 'miracle chicken', which hatches out in a human armpit before clucking off to find its victim – nowhere near as tempting as the human dupe version, and you have to keep it busy or it will trash your house). The Trauco of the Chiloé Province, Chile, is a rather more inviting prospect – a sexually powerful and irresistible forest creature who is said to seduce any attractive young woman, leaving her utterly unable to resist his advances. Many an unexpected pregnancy has been blamed on the potency of the Trauco.

The attraction of the incubus and succubus legends lies in the fact that their will cannot be denied – they forcibly remove our moral code, meaning we cannot be expected to take responsibility for our actions while in their thrall. Which is handy.

Augustin Calmet's eighteenth-century work on the occult, already mentioned in chapter one, includes many fascinatingly titled topics on an array of esoteric subjects. Few are more intriguing than chapter eight – '*Prodigious effects of Imagination in those Men or Women who believe they hold Intercourse with the Demon.*' In this, Calmet argues that physical connection is impossible between humans and either angels or demons, for the simple reason that the latter are 'purely spiritual substances'. On this basis, he also declares that any claim to have had 'personal intercourse' with such a creature must be the product of a 'depraved or deranged imagination'. He goes on to describe instances in which people claimed to have been seduced by said apparitions, including a young woman who believed she was being visited by a 'gentleman of good family', who took advantage of her gullibility and ensuing trust in his promises of marriage. It was several months before the girl discovered that the gentleman in question had actually been out of town at the time of the supposed proposal. She was rewarded for her mistreatment, Calmet informs us, by being dispatched to a nunnery in order to do 'penance for her double crime'.

One has to wonder whether the young lady's secret visitor was, in fact, the person she believed it to be all along, and perhaps the rather ungentlemanly gentleman used the beliefs of a more credulous time to persuade the girl that she had, indeed, been victim of demonic seduction. Regardless, the fault was of course laid squarely at the feet of the young woman herself, who was removed from polite society forthwith.

Social and moral mores in the nineteenth and early twentieth century being what they were, it was all but impossible for anyone – particularly women – to be openly sexual. Thus the vampire protagonist in popular literature takes away such a dilemma, by simply forcing him- or herself upon their victims, invariably in an attractively seductive manner. The intimacy of an encounter with a vampire is often reinforced by physical attraction to someone who would otherwise be out of bounds. This occasionally appears to be a deliberate move on the part of an author who is perhaps diverting their personal desires safely into print.

Bram Stoker was 50 years old when he wrote *Dracula* in 1897. Published during an era in which libidinous desires were hidden away underneath layers of societal politeness, the Count is the archetypal antihero. Despite his psychopathic lack of empathy for human life – and an unnerving tendency to turn into terrifying creatures in order to escape from those who would hunt him down – we cannot help but feel some level of empathy for the tragedy of his character. The Count has spent centuries in near isolation in the depths of Carpathia, polishing his hatred of the human race to a gleaming black shine. But even at its driest, most straightforward moments, *Dracula* is all about desire. Poor mad Renfield, desperate for a kitten, wants to eat it and literally take it inside himself in the same way as he's done with the creepy crawlies roaming the bare floors of his cell. He, too, is mad with desire – even though it is in essence a desire to serve his master.

Much has been made of Keanu Reeves's acting – or lack thereof – in *Bram Stoker's Dracula*. It cannot be denied that in this interpretation of the Dracula story, Jonathan Harker is often more wooden than the stakes Van Helsing takes with him on a vampire hunt. But it's one of Harker's scenes that still sticks like a rush of fresh O-negative in the minds of many who have seen the film.

While investigating the castle, Harker comes upon a heavy, unlocked door, which leads into a room dominated by a spread of flowing sheets and cushions on the floor in the manner of a fairy-tale harem (albeit one with rather more dust and cobwebs than one might usually expect). Guided by what he believes to be Mina's whispering voice, Harker sits on the bed and watches mesmerised as an invisible weight makes footprints in the soft floor. As the mesmerised Harker falls backwards on the bed, a beautiful, bejewelled woman rises slowly from the floor, sliding up between his legs in the manner of a hungry serpent. The sensual eroticism in this scene emanates from the screen in waves, mostly down to Monica Belucci's mesmerisingly voluptuous appearance. Luckily for Reeves's vampiric acting technique, Harker is required to do very little other than gasp helplessly as he is seduced first by Belucci and then also by her fellow undead seductresses. The colouration of the scene changes from near-sepia to a deep, glowing blood red as the women make it very clear that they are hungry for Harker – and not just in a metaphorical sense.

As their attentions become more urgent, Harker belatedly realises the danger he is in – but it's too late. The women attack, one in particular getting her fangs close enough to his groin to make him sit up in fright. We see Harker in a ceiling mirror, writhing around apparently alone, his tormentors invisible in the silvered glass. The women drink from him, lasciviously licking and kissing both their victim and each other, toying with Harker as though they were cats and he a particularly tasty mouse. Their murderous orgy is only halted when Dracula flies into the room, raging at them and shouting that Harker belongs to him. The women scuttle away across the walls and ceilings like monstrous human insects as Dracula berates them.

One of the women hisses at the Count, 'You, yourself, have never loved,' to which he retorts, 'Yes, I too can love. And I shall love again.' It is phrased as a threat, rather than an explanation or answer. The women are by now crawling around Dracula's feet, cats suddenly transformed into hungry kittens begging for food. Their master has brought them a baby, which, to Harker's abject horror, they fall upon with hungry glee. In this scene – as with many in this particular adaptation – blood and lust are as one. But the lust is on Harker's side and the blood is the domain of the vampires that would seduce him in order to drink him dry.

Back in England, Mina Murray receives her fiancé's letter, advising that he will be away for a month. She is perching on the edge of an ornamental pond in a light, bright flower garden which wouldn't look out of place in Wonderland. One almost expects Tweedledum and Tweedledee to pop out from behind a rose bush as Mina frets, delicately – a vision in pale green taffeta that is a direct and intentional contrast to her husband's nightmarish plight. But Mina's worries are about to multiply even further.

As Mina explains her concerns about Jonathan to Lucy, a storm hits without warning. A ghostly, ghastly vision of Dracula appears in the clouds and the scene cuts abruptly to the friends kissing passionately in the rain, apropos of apparently nothing except for the purpose of looking hot in dripping wet frocks. The storm intensifies and we see snapshots of the madness taking hold – animals in London Zoo becoming agitated, a wolf making its escape, Tom Waits playing Renfield to the max as the most Tom Waits character ever seen in a Victorian asylum. Mina later discovers that Lucy has walked out of her room in the middle of the night in some form of trance, her crucifix left discarded on her pillow and spots her wandering the ornamental, maze-like garden. For some unspecified reason now dressed in a billowing gown in blood orange colours, Lucy is chased by a panicking Mina, whose voluptuously naked form is clearly shown under her floaty pale nightgown as she bounces after her friend. As Lucy walks confidently towards her doom, Mina flails after her through the maze, a pale wraith in the moonlight. The scene in which Mina stands shocked and frozen at the sight of her friend being raped by the Count in monstrous form is almost comedic, despite its awful subject matter. He is first drawn by the blood pulsing in Mina's veins but is then horrified that the person he truly desires has seen him in his most animalistic form. He solves this socially awkward situation by simply ordering 'Do not see me!' before disappearing, leaving Mina to gather up her hurt and confused friend and take her back to the supposed safety of the house. What Mina doesn't yet realise is that it is already too late – poor Lucy is now well on her way to becoming another creature of the night, doomed by her own sexuality.

Offered a glimpse into the pure passion and animal lust that clearly isn't in Jonathan Harker's repertoire, Mina is pulled into the Count's web like an all too willing fly. Winona Ryder plays Mina as opposing characters – one sexual, the other innocently fragile. Her blossoming desire for the Count overrides her repulsion at hearing that he was responsible for so much death and destruction, including the death of Lucy Westenra. Leaning forward to suck at the wound on his chest, her behaviour is nothing like that of the prim young woman she was at the start of the story.

Dracula's 'brides' make a reappearance in the story as our merry band of vampire hunters chase the Count back to his lair in the hope of destroying him once and for all. No matter how desperately Van Helsing attempts to protect Mina as they wait in the snow outside Dracula's castle, her connection to the Count only strengthens. Encouraged by the spectral Brides, she moves in to seduce her guardian, loosening her clothes lasciviously and murmuring of how Lucy harboured secret desires for the older man. As he is lured in, Mina suddenly snaps into a gloating, murderous fury. 'Will you cut off my head and drive a stake through my heart,' she asks in a coquettish voice, 'as you did poor Lucy? You murdering bastard!'

It's only when she launches in for the kill, fangs at the ready, that her previously willing would-be victim comes to his senses. Utilising his ready supply of religious quotations along with a handy stash of communion wafers, Van Helsing manages to ward off danger – for now, at least. And lo – the man of God has once again saved the poor female from the consequences of her own desires. If the moralising wasn't already clear enough, Van Helsing waits for the protection afforded him by daylight to go after Dracula's harem. 'Whores of Satan!' he cries, beheading them one at a time in their undead sleep. Grasping their heads by the hair, he carries them like game, as though they're the catch from a good day's hunting. Van Helsing throws them casually off the cliff, nothing more than garbage.

As previously mentioned, Coppola's interpretation is not a faithful rendering of Bram Stoker's original story, despite the implication held within its title. The Count's tragic wife Elisabeta is an entirely new character that was written in by Coppola and screenwriter James V. Hart and, in this version, the loss of Elisabeta is the reasoning for Dracula becoming a vampire in the first place. Rather than being bitten and 'turned' by an older vamp, the Count turns *himself* through the sheer force of his grief and rage as he denounces the church for rejecting his lost love on the grounds of her suicide (a rarely mentioned side note about the movie is that Oldman's screaming was deemed too weak for such a powerful scene – the anguished voice we hear is actually that of musician Lux Interior from The Cramps) .

Elisabeta then acts as the thread pulling Dracula and Mina closer together as the story develops. Although it is never explicitly stated, the clear implication is that Mina is the reincarnation of Elisabeta – or at least, carries something of Elisabeta's spirit and memories with her. It is Mina who finally 'saves' Dracula, killing him in order to finally give his spirit the release it has long craved. The chapel she has dragged him into appears to be the same one in which Elisabeta's body was laid after she was recovered from the Danube. As Dracula now finds the peace that has eluded him for so long, we see that the painting on the chapel ceiling now shows the pair reunited.

At heart a tale of true love being stronger than life – or death – itself, *Bram Stoker's Dracula* is as heavy on the moralising as it is on the glossy special effects. Its luxuriantly gothic scenery is the perfect background for one of the simplest stories of all time – good versus evil and love above all. But one is left with an uneasy feeling that perhaps, when all is said and done, it's not so easy to decide which side is which.

Stoker was possibly using *Dracula* to make sense of more personal desires in a time when to do so publicly would have brought public and absolute disgrace. Married to Florence Balcombe, Oscar Wilde's childhood sweetheart – Wilde was said to be distraught when Balcombe chose Stoker over himself – Stoker stayed in touch with Wilde through their adult lives, standing by the disgraced writer through his prison sentence and eventual self imposed exile (Stoker was one of the few people who visited Wilde in Paris after his release from prison). Stoker had what we would today think of as crushes on other men at various points throughout his life. He worked with Henry Irving at the Lyceum Theatre off the Strand in central London for decades, first as acting manager and then as business manager from 1878 to 1898 (Stoker was still working at the theatre when *Dracula* was published). Despite both men being married to society beauties, theirs appears to have been a very close relationship – albeit one treasured more by Stoker than by Irving, who didn't always treat Stoker well.

The most notable focus of Stoker's affections was, however, Walt Whitman, the renowned American poet. Whitman was widely assumed to be homosexual, a theory that was only reinforced by such works as *Leaves of Grass*, a collection of poetry noted for its openness about the joys of sensual pleasure and the beauty of the human form.

> I sing the body electric,
> The armies of those I love engirth me and I engirth them,
> They will not let me off till I go with them, respond to them,
> And discorrupt them, and charge them full with the charge
>     of the soul.
>
> Was it doubted that those who corrupt their own bodies
>     conceal themselves?
> And if those who defile the living are as bad as they who
>     defile the dead?
> And if the body does not do fully as much as the soul?
> And if the body were not the soul, what is the soul?
>
> From 'I Sing The Body Electric' by Walt Whitman, 1855.
> Originally untitled, included in *Leaves of Grass*.

Interestingly, in 1912 Stoker declared that all homosexual authors ought to be imprisoned, in a move that some historians see as a smokescreen aimed at covering his own, then illicit, desires. There is also some argument that Stoker's cause of death in Pimlico on 20 April 1912 was not one which would usually be expected of a man of his moral standing. Called to give the cause of death for the purpose of registering with the coroner, Dr James Browne attested that Stoker had been suffering from, among other more prosaic ailments, 'locomotor ataxia, 6 months'. Locomotor ataxia is an infection in the spinal cord that causes loss of coordination of movement. The degeneration of the spinal nerves that brings on such symptoms can have various causes but was most often caused by venereal disease. In the early twentieth century, using the term 'locomotor ataxia' on a death certificate was, more often than not, a polite way of saying that a person was suffering from tertiary – late stage – syphilis.

It is difficult, at more than a century's distance, to say for certain what Bram Stoker's motives were; either in writing such a direct story about the battle between good and evil, love and lust, or in the presumed behaviour that – as well as clearly being far from the moralistic purity he appeared to prize so highly – may have led to his own appointment with death. For one thing, it might well not have been the cause – Stoker was apparently capable of writing and dealing with paperwork until almost the very end of his life, an ability that was unlikely to be present in someone dying of syphilis, with all the mental degeneration it invariably entailed. But it cannot be denied that the helplessness portrayed in vampire stories legitimises those fantasies that we might otherwise be too scared to consider – something that is even more important in cultures where straying from the accepted sexual norm could lead to being ostracised or even killed.

Stoker had witnessed his close friend Wilde brought to his knees by the British legal system purely because of Wilde's sexual inclinations. Liberal MP Henry Labouchère last minute amendment to the 1885 Criminal Amendment Act had resulted in the addition of a section – within an Act which was intended for the protection of women and children – which criminalised homosexuality among men. It was a wide-ranging remit, specified only as 'gross indecency', which had no accompanying limits or contexts to give guidance as to how it might be interpreted. In effect, any man could be accused of and prosecuted for the 'crime' of being homosexual, purely on the suspicion of any third party. And of course, the accuser might have reasons of their own to want to blacken the name of another man.

Given the threat of social ostracism and legal battles, it isn't difficult to understand why Stoker might perhaps have sublimated his own desires into his monstrous creation. The Count cared not one jot for the whims of polite society – he knew what he wanted and took it, regardless of his victim's gender. There must have been a kind of freedom for Stoker in living through the Count's fictional existence – an existence in which bloodlust and sexuality came to the fore and in which the identity of who was 'good' and who was 'bad' is often rather ambiguous. Could Stoker's tale of lost love, death and visceral passion have been his way of channelling unspoken desires? We will never know for sure. It is dangerous to view past situations through the lens of our current worldview, with all the differences in accepted morality that comes with it. Stoker may not have even understood his own desires enough to have ever verbalised them, but one doesn't need to be a psychoanalyst to see that they're there, simmering away just a fraction beneath the surface.

Sex and death are two of the only certainties in life (taxes seemingly being an optional extra for many sections of society these days). Regardless of our own personal beliefs, we are all a result of sex in some form (even if it is as impersonal and basic as a sperm and an egg being introduced in a test tube, the mechanics of the process still have their roots in the physical act) and we will all die. This leaves us with a tangled web of emotions and desires, many of which are subconscious but still cling together like magnets in ways that some find uncomfortable. It's no coincidence that the most popular of the vampire stories are those which portray death as an almost sexual act – the visceral intimacy involved in both makes it impossible for them to be separated at an animalistic level. We are fascinated by those who allow themselves the freedom to fully experience both the sex act and that of killing (mostly) without guilt. Guilt is a driving force in society and an escape from it is always welcome – as long as that escape is within the realms of fiction.

As humans, we rarely get to indulge our deepest darkest desires. Those desires don't have to be directly related to wanting to commit an abhorrent act, but we're fascinated by those who do. And we want to know *why*. The most mild mannered of grandmothers might be obsessed with true crime stories – it's unlikely that she herself is ever going to murder someone, but she escapes into a world where people can and do the things she most fears. Facing our demons makes us feel safer. Learning about something that scares us gives us a false impression of security, a false sense of control in a world where very few of us are absolutely in control of our lives. Many of us lack the financial wherewithal to do whatever we please, or we have commitments that we can't (or don't wish to) drop responsibility for.

It's no wonder then that the vampire, with its ability to take what it wants without guilt or shame, is such a powerful figure in so many people's fantasies. Our sexuality has been bounded by societal rules and regulations since time immemorial, our behaviour restricted by tenets set by those more powerful than ourselves. Vampires don't care for rules. If they want something, they have it without considering the consequences, because in most cases there *are* no consequences. A vampire is, in effect, humanity distilled to its most animalistic essence – a creature that kills and steals and feeds without compunction. Mere mortals, on the other hand, are subject to the whims and wishes of others. If we don't follow the crowd we risk being ostracised, and being out of step with society can be dangerous.

Lucy Westenra rails against society's rules in *Dracula*, complaining to her friend Mina of the restrictions put upon her for the crime of simply being female. 'Why can't they let a girl marry three men, or as many as want her?' she asks. She's not quite serious about it, but one gets the distinct impression that Lucy would certainly prefer it to be an option. Lucy loves life, and loves people, and loves men – in a manner that is restrained in comparison to modern times, but certainly more open than would have been socially acceptable in the late nineteenth century. Of course, being restricted by social mores didn't negate love and desire in the 1800s any more than it does today, whether in literature or in reality. Sexual desire is an innate part of human nature and as such it cannot ever be completely controlled by social rules and regulations. There is good reason why 'sensation novels' that caused such a stir in the latter half of the nineteenth century were so popular – people have always loved to be shocked and titillated, regardless of the era in which they lived. Humans have always desired, and they've always been good at hiding that desire by siphoning it off into less risky outlets. Vampires have been used as a metaphor for forbidden passions ever since Lord Ruthven seduced his first victim. They are the perfect fantasy fodder – otherworldly, above the law and above retribution. They tempt us into the things that we want to do, but are too scared to try.

A 'good' girl – and it is, usually, women and girls who are evaluated in this way – has been judged negatively throughout time for being sexual. But if that woman were to be seduced by a being more powerful than herself – a creature that was too strong for her to fight off, for example – then she has an excuse for her actions. There's a reason why powerful and commandeering men make up so many of the 'hero' roles in romantic 'bodice-ripping' novels – and a reason why the bodice needs to be ripped in the first place. Being overpowered is a very common fantasy, and not a new one. Even though the 'vampire as well dressed, seductive villain' is a relatively new invention, the early years of his existence was still a time when desire wasn't spoken of openly for fear of being seen to 'cheapen' oneself in some way. Female value was based on innocence and purity. But the imagination is a powerful thing and it is unsurprising that first Lord Ruthven, then Carmilla and finally Count Dracula caught the collective imaginations of an outwardly prim nineteenth-century society. This theme was reinforced further with the advent of film. Now audiences could see 'real' vampires seducing poor innocent maidens, and squeal politely in horror at such scenes while almost certainly thinking 'but what if?' in their minds. Even the monstrous Nosferatu, all fangs and claws, prowls in the manner of an animal looking to make a kill. By the time we get to Christopher Lee's portrayal of Count Dracula, the sexuality is overt. His victims are beautiful and blessed with heaving bosoms, and – more importantly – they get to be seduced most glamorously while also appearing to be desperately clinging to their innocence. Outward appearances are the important thing, after all.

The trope of the devilishly attractive 'bad boy' (or girl) is an old one – for many, there is nothing quite like the temptation of someone you know in your heart of hearts would be absolutely terrible for you. Lord Byron was labelled as 'mad, bad and dangerous to know' by Lady Caroline Lamb back in 1812, a phrase which has gone down in history as the poet's unofficial epitaph. It has been alleged in some quarters that part of his reasoning behind ending their subsequent affair was that he simply couldn't keep up with her, either emotionally or physically. Regardless of the veracity of said rumours, the couple's brief liaison was notoriously tumultuous – it inspired much debate and has filled endless pages of academic discourse ever since. Perhaps the most interesting thing to note is that they clearly sparked each other's lust for life (and lust for, well, just about everything else). We might not ourselves wish to be in such a tempestuous relationship, but one can't help envy – just a little bit – the sheer overwhelming powers of emotion that must have been involved.

Most of us lead relatively drab and boring lives on a day-to-day level. Societal and financial constraints mean that, where our cave-dwelling ancestors once spent their days fighting to survive, we spend a lot of time worrying about bills and wondering whether we really want to be with that long-term partner we've had for years (when deep in our hearts we know that really we're just tolerating them out of habit). We spend so much time just *existing*, that the idea of being seduced by someone who wants us at a purely visceral level of animalistic need is escapism at its finest.

*Vampire Lovers* (dir. Roy Ward Baker, 1970), is an adaptation of Sheridan Le Fanu's *Carmilla*. A joint British American production between Hammer Film Productions and American International, the film starred Ingrid Pitt as Marcilla/Carmilla/Mircalla. Although the adaptation plays fast and loose with the original story, the main characters are kept (in this version, our vampiric protagonist also appears to be immune to daylight – when it suits her). After her mother leaves her in the care of

General Spielsdorf and his daughter Laura, Marcilla seduces the sweetly innocent girl and gradually drains her of life. Making a rapid exit after Laura's death, the newly renamed Carmilla then moves in on Emma, whose governess rapidly falls for Carmilla's charms and becomes her all-too-willing accomplice.

Despite having been written with the explicit intent of taking advantage of the relaxation of both film censorship and public perception of on-screen sexuality, *Vampire Lovers* is incredibly tame by modern standards. For a film that includes so much nudity, it somehow manages to radiate an air of innocence. Some of the dialogue falls flat and many of the actors appear to have forgotten that they were supposed to change their facial expressions as they spoke. Nevertheless, both Ingrid Pitt and Peter Cushing give sterlingly hammy performances. *Vampire Lovers* is well worth watching for anyone with a taste for old school, 'blood and bosoms' horror.

'Animalistic need' is certainly one way of describing the (sometimes rather tenuous) plot lines in the 1999 anthology *In Blood We Lust*, published in the UK by Dark Angel Press. It's hardly surprising that vampires should have found themselves the theme of an entire collection of (extremely graphic) erotica – after all, a vampire is about as visceral as it's possible to get. The thirty-three stories included in this particular collection are unusual in that they are almost all composed as if vampires were writing erotica for themselves. *In Blood We Lust* sees the undead as the righteous protagonists who are simply following their instincts, regardless of the depravity into which it leads.

Mental assault, rape, sex with hermaphroditic vampire mutants – it's all here. Even necrophilia (I consulted the social media hive mind while writing this book, to check whether people still considered it necrophilia if the person doing the deed was themselves dead – the general consensus was that yes, it is). Never has the phrase 'if you can think it, someone's already made porn of it' been so apt. The interesting thing about *In Blood We Lust* is that, according to the introduction, it is written from a 'pro-vampire stance' – as if vampires were themselves writing for an audience of their own kind. General squeamishness aside, there is something refreshing about stories that don't even begin to pretend to constrain themselves within the usual moral and ethical standards one would expect from even the cheapest and most graphic erotic literature. From an academic viewpoint, while the majority of the stories are faintly repulsive rather than being in any way 'sexy', they also raise some interesting questions about humanity's more base urges. Does turning them into fictional entertainment makes them in any way more acceptable on a hypothetical fantasy level?

One thing's for sure – if *In Blood We Lust* really was aiming at the genuine vampire market then it would certainly succeed, because it graphically illustrates just how viscerally grim a vampire's sex life might be.

Laurell K. Hamilton's 'Anita Blake, Vampire Hunter' series has sold millions of books since the first instalment, *Guilty Pleasures*, was published in 1993. A fairly standard trope in itself – a paid killer living in parallel universe almost identical to our own, but with supernatural creatures existing alongside humans – Hamilton's series stands out for both the depth of the writing and the solid world-building around her eponymous lead character. Anita Blake is a professional vampire hunter and zombie raiser, working in a legitimised role alongside the police force of St Louis, Missouri. Blake is, in effect, a legitimised murderer – a role made all the more morally uncertain by the fact that she often has to make her own decisions as to whether a potential target is genuinely guilty and deserving of a final death.

Blake's attitude changes across the series – from a hard-nosed vampire killer at the beginning, into someone who, while perhaps not ever likely to trust vamps entirely, certainly isn't averse to getting both emotionally and physically entwined with them. There has been some dissent from sections of Hamilton's fanbase who were concerned about the increasing levels of eroticism as the series progressed, and there's certainly no denying that the sexual element becomes both more overt and more graphic over time. But isn't this why most readers of vampire fiction are attracted to such books in the first place? Discounting the occasional bloodsucking book for children, most tales of the undead have some level of physical attraction at their heart. And Blake deals with things on her own terms wherever possible, as a fully autonomous and independent woman.

Long before *Twilight* became the number one obsession of everyone in love with glossy, rich vampires, Poppy Z. Brite's *Lost Souls* was the vampire myth of choice for a generation of confused teens. First published in 1992, it tells the story of Nothing, a teenage vampire searching for … something. In Brite's world, vampires are a species unto themselves and therefore unconstrained by the restrictions usually faced by the creatures of the night. They can breed with humans, but when the unborn baby comes to term it chews its way out of its mother, killing her in the process. The same trope would later be used by Meyer in *Breaking Dawn*, the last in the *Twilight* series, but not with the same levels of gore that is used in *Lost Souls*. Teenage (human) girl Jessy, pregnant by nomadic vampire Zillah, dies in childbirth – an event so brilliantly bloody that it is capable of putting most people off having sex for a very long time after reading it. Her son, Nothing, is adopted and raised by an unwitting couple who love and cosset him to the point that he escapes just as soon as he can. His journey to find some answers in his life brings the threads of different stories crashing together in a tangle of human/vampire confusion.

Brite's vampires don't even pretend to follow the moral codes so beloved of humanity – and neither do many of the humans. There's rape, incest, murder (obviously) and a very 1990s love of the music of The Cure and Bauhaus. But rather than coming across as a tasteless exercise in shock horror, Brite's characters are portrayed with a deep level of understanding that makes them more palatable – even lovable. Yes, they commit unspeakable atrocities, but we can see how – and, more importantly, *why* – such events occur. Logic is twisted in order to fit the story, with Nothing ageing pretty much normally until he reaches his late teens, where he appears to stall. Of course, the ageing process of vampires differs with pretty much each new interpretation, each one of which reworks all the old ideas and adds a few new ones, in order to fit the ideas of its author.

One could argue that the most romantic attachment in *Lost Souls* is that between Steve and Ghost, the human men who make up the eponymous group of the book's title and between whom there is an almost constant air of homoeroticism. Their relationship doesn't develop past the platonic in this book – although it does in the sort-of sequel, Brite's short story *Stay Awake* – and it is sometimes uncomfortable. It is a particular issue for Steve, who considers himself the epitome of masculinity and struggles with his own thoughts and feelings when they don't quite do as he thinks they should. Written before the age of the modern internet – and long before the advent of social media – *Lost Souls* is a story very much of its time. Whether or not it is up there with the greatest vampire stories ever written is open to debate, but it is definitely one of the most interesting. Its author certainly understood 'otherness'. Poppy Z. Brite is now Billy

Martin, having transitioned in the years since writing *Lost Souls*. Martin has spoken publicly of how he struggled with gender dysphoria from a young age, describing himself as having been 'a gay man who happens to have been born in a female body'. This is perhaps where Martin/ Brite's depth of characterisation comes from – he has clearly been able to envisage many of the different angles of gender perspective from an early age.

> There comes a time, for every vampire, when the idea of eternity becomes, momentarily, unbearable. Living in the shadows, feeding in the darkness, with only your own company to keep, rots into a solitary, hollow existence. Immortality seems like a good idea – until you realise you're going to spend it alone.
>
> From *Queen of the Damned*,
> dir. Michael Rymer, 2002.

*Queen of the Damned* was the 2002 (very loose) adaption of the third book in Anne Rice's *The Vampire Chronicles* series. Lestat is back – and this time he's a rock star. Of course he is – the glamorous, nocturnal, endlessly exciting life of the cliched rock musician is the perfect occupation for an undead thrill-seeker. As Lestat himself says, 'It became worthwhile to rise again, as new gods were born and worshipped. Night and day, they were never alone. I would become one of them.'

Probably best known for being the last movie appearance by American singer and actress Aaliyah, who was killed in a plane crash just prior to its release, this isn't the best vampire film ever. It's not even a particularly *good* film. But what it lacks in finesse, *Queen of the Damned* makes up for with sheer visceral sexuality of the kind found in the dark corners of cheap nightclubs and at the bottom of empty bourbon glasses.

The 2020 Gatiss and Moffat adaptation of *Dracula* for the BBC was broadcast just as I was finishing writing this book, so I watched with a perhaps more cynically clinical eye than most viewers. What struck me forcibly is that however innovative the adaptation was, at the heart of it – possibly even more so than in the many previous versions that have been released over the past century – was one man as the embodiment of darkness, evil and, more than anything, lust. This Dracula, played by

Claes Bang, is a tightly coiled spring, hunting out sex (of a kind), blood and power with a dark and powerful passion. Charming and personable, the Count chats casually about his demonic plans with the light-hearted jokiness of an East End wide boy, toying with his victims in the way a cat plays with a mouse before finally getting bored enough to kill it. His casual cruelty comes out in some of the sharpest one liners. When the doomed Jonathan Harker exclaims, 'You're a monster!' Dracula replies drily, 'You're a lawyer. Nobody's perfect.'

For once, the details which are changed work with the script, rather than against it. Characters are played around with – notably in the case of Mina, who relatively brief appearance portrays her as an almost chimeric mix of her original character and that of Lucy Westenra, a mixture of shy prettiness and naked passion. When she writes to Jonathan at the beginning of the story, she talks of not blaming him should he be unfaithful and how she has plenty of male attention to keep her busy while he is away attending to the mysterious Count's affairs. The Count's own sexuality is referenced obliquely early on, when Sister Agatha Van Helsing asks Jonathan if he has had sex with the Count. And indeed, Dracula is sexual towards almost *everything* – physical lust appears to be as much a part of him as the bloodlust that drives his hunt. But writer Moffat warned viewers not to take this aspect of the Count's personality too literally, declaring in an interview with *The Times* in December 2019 that, 'He's bi-homicidal, it's not the same thing […] He's killing them, not dating them.' Speaking to *The Telegraph*, he went on, 'He's not actually having sex with anyone. He's drinking their blood. […]Dracula has always fed off men and women.'

Agatha Van Helsing is a wonder – so changed from the Van Helsing of the original book, yet a fully fleshed and worthy character in herself. The cynical nun, played by Dolly Wells, describes vampirism matter-of-factly as 'a contagion' which removes 'the holy ability to die'. When asked by Dracula why she is in a convent, given that she clearly doesn't believe in God, Agatha replies drily, 'Like many women my age, I am trapped in a loveless marriage, maintaining appearances for the sake of a roof over my head.' There is always something of a confused dichotomy around an attractive nun, especially one who is highly intelligent and not afraid to show it. As Agatha herself says to the Count as he prowls the perimeter of St Mary's convent, 'I'm all your nightmares at once – an intelligent woman with a crucifix.'

Agatha isn't a conventional nun by any means – if anything, she's only one short step away from being an atheist – but she's as fascinated by Dracula as any woman has ever been in the history of the myth. Agatha's difference is that, rather than adopting the usual 'rabbit in headlights' expression beloved of female characters/victims in previous adaptations, she herself is, in many ways, the predator. Agatha hunts Dracula – not necessarily the man himself, but the truth and logic (or lack thereof) behind his self-made myth. She has developed theories about him that she's not afraid to test out, even when she's not entirely sure she's right. This is a nun who is almost too clever for her own good, simply because she can't stop herself *wondering*. Agatha has become bored with religion, disillusioned with her god and now has found a far more interesting target on which to focus her beady eyes.

When Agatha is taken into a dream world as Dracula feeds from her, she is less nun and more woman. Her hair is loose and gloriously flowing and she is playing her captor at chess with a sharp eye and a determination to beat him. She still wears her usual nun's habit, but now it comes across as being a flowing dress, rather than a utilitarian means to cover the female form. As the realisation of her true predicament begins to dawn on Agatha, the expression on her face becomes one of anguished dismay, rather than fear or anger.

Rather than the doomed romantic hero so often reimagined over the years, Moffat and Gatiss present the Count as a creature that has lost all shreds of humanity. Dracula isn't an almost-human antihero that one can feel sympathy for – he is an animal, pure and simple. This bloodsucker hasn't lost his empathy for humans, because he never had it in the first place. Animals, babies, nuns – they're all just a potential walking buffet to this creature of the night. But sexuality exudes from Claes Bang's performance – this Dracula is hotter than the depths of hell, even while evil shines more brightly from him than the sun he believes he'll never see again (interestingly, Stoker didn't imply that daylight could kill vampires – that particular kryptonite began with Murnau's *Nosferatu*). He politely asks Jonathan to describe the sunrise to him, as he lies down next to the dying man in a gesture of intimacy more familiar to lovers than between a killer and his victim. References to previous incarnations of the most famous vampire of them all flash by almost in the blink of an eye. When Harker first realises the awful truth, the Count's eyes redden and his fangs leer out at us in an almost perfect replica of the pose struck so famously by Christopher Lee in 1958. Parts of the 2020 adaptation were, in fact, filmed at Bray Studios in Berkshire. Famous for its association with the Hammer horror movies franchise, Bray was the place where Lee gave the performance which sealed Dracula in the public consciousness, more than fifty years earlier.

Critical reaction to this reimagining of the myth was split fairly evenly between those who absolutely adored it and those who thought the writers should be burned at the stake for taking such liberties with an old and beloved script. The latter, in my view at least, missed the point entirely. *Dracula* is, and always has been, a metaphor. The subject of that metaphor changes with almost every adaptation, but it was always a story about something far bigger than the sum of its parts. Stoker was a complicated character whose true self was quite possibly completely different to the character he presented in public – and the characters in his creation are the same. In both the original and the adaptation, Van Helsing is the embodiment of science, patriarchy and a mixture of modern thinking and the Old Ways. S/he is clinging to their beliefs as if to a life raft, while knowing that there is every chance they will be thrown off into the sea of unbelievers and left to fend for themselves.

And Count Dracula himself? He is all of us – our innermost desires and dreams and fears, pulled together and brought to life in an overwhelming mixture of terror and lust. We want him as much as we want to *be* him.

This particular adaptation humanises Dracula as much as it demonises him. If anything, Claes Bang's turn as the Count is hotter precisely *because* he is just so utterly awful. This Drac doesn't even have to take his trousers off to give the ladies – or men– the ride of their life. His sensuality comes from the power of his personality and the sense that one really is in the presence of something that, while it might look like a man, is, in truth, utterly inhuman.

Which is precisely what attracts the modern-day Lucy Westenra. This version of Lucy is a party girl who loves attention and loves men – but only if they never love her back. Lucy doesn't want commitments or obligations or anything other than sweet, blissful oblivion – and Dracula can give her that in spades. The more he takes, the more she offers – and the more fascinated with her he becomes. Dracula has never met anyone like Lucy in all his centuries of existence – someone who is truly unafraid of death. In that, she is stronger than him – and he knows it, even if he would never admit it. Because of her lack of fear, Lucy gives herself willingly and is prepared to take things far further than is safe – but she's doing it for her own reasons, not because she's scared of Dracula or trying to impress him. The biggest difference in this version of Stoker's story is that the women are by far the stronger characters.

*True Blood*'s Sookie Stackhouse is similar to Sister Agatha in that she's not scared when she meets her first vampire – if anything, she's excited. Sookie knows what it is to be an outsider and is confident enough in herself to take calculated risks. *True Blood* gives a new take on some old vampire tropes. According to Bill Compton, it was in vampires' interests to establish fake myths about themselves early on. When Sookie questions the fact that she can see his reflection in the mirror, he explains that 'if humans thought that we couldn't be seen in a mirror, it was another way for us to prove that we weren't vampires and that way we could stay hidden.' Ditto holy water – 'just water' – and crucifixes. 'Geometry', Bill explains, with a dismissive wave of his hand. Garlic is the one thing with some relationship to reality, in Bill's world, 'it's irritating, but that's pretty much it.' In one short scene, Compton dismisses pretty much every vampire trope that has ever existed. Which only serves to make the vampires of Bon Temps all the more unnerving, because until they show their fangs, it's often impossible to tell who's human and who's a walking, talking, member of the undead. Blood and sex are wrapped tightly around each other in Sookie's world, their intimacy intertwined and myths overturned.

In our modern world, blood is often portrayed as a potential killer, spreading disease and misery between those who are foolish enough to exchange bodily fluids. We have learned to avoid contact with the blood of others to avoid risk of contamination, often for very good reason. *True Blood* uses blood differently. In Sookie's universe, vampire blood is directly related to sex in a positive way, rather than negative. It carries no danger to the humans who consume it other than the very real risk of becoming addicted to its powers. The value of 'V' as an intense aphrodisiac for humans means that it rapidly becomes highly prized. Indeed, in a reversal of usual roles, some vampires fall victim to human hunters looking to make a literal killing out of their undead vital essence.

Sookie risks her life saving Bill from the Rattray's in episode one of the first series of *True Blood*. Hard as nails and with the morals of particularly devious alley cats, Denise and Mack Rattray, realising that Bill is a vampire, immediately plan to steal his blood to sell on the black market. Having read their thoughts in the diner, Sookie knows that Bill is in serious danger and decides that she has no option but to help him (but not before wrapping a silver chain around her neck – Sookie might be naive, but she's no idiot). Sookie survives the ensuing bloody fight, but only by drinking some of Bill's blood for its healing properties. Initially repulsed, she eventually drinks at Bill's insistence, her disgust turning to eagerness as his blood enters her body.

When she wakes the next day, Sookie finds that her human senses have heightened to an unnerving degree. Her strength increases, as does her power of sight and hearing. Her sense of smell is such that she sniffs out a tiny crumb of food that has become trapped under furniture in her grandmother's immaculate house. Bill is also open about the potential benefits to Sookie's sex life, should she continue to drink from him. It's easy to see why, in the *True Blood* universe, vampire blood is such a valuable commodity to those who are mortal and therefore inherently weak – many of us would be tempted to try out superpowers, even just for a short while (although the sight of Sookie's well-meaning but wayward brother Jason having to have excessive blood drained from his penis in one memorable scene after overdoing the 'V-juice' is probably enough to make most people resign themselves to being 100% mortal).

Once described by esteemed film critic Roger Ebert as 'an agonisingly bad vampire movie, circling around an exquisitely effective sex scene', *The Hunger* is certainly on the slow side (and all the more beautiful for it). But there's no questioning the fact that the scene Ebert refers to is the one that sticks in most viewers' minds.

Human Sarah spills her drink down the t-shirt under which she clearly wears no bra, and we immediately cut to her sponging it down very slowly, while vampire Miriam watches. The sensuality of the ensuing sexual encounter isn't up for question – it's carefully written and beautifully shot in a way that makes it far less sensationalist than most lesbian encounters one sees in big budget movies. Miriam is sitting at the piano playing the *Flower Duet* from *Lakmé* by Leo Delibes, which is taken up by the movie's soundtrack as the women move to the bedroom. Their movements are so languorous, the slow writhing given its own soft focus by the floating voile drapes around which the camera peeks, that the viewer becomes lulled into a false sense of security. The low tone that begins to pulse through the music is the only signifier that things are not going to end as romantically as they began.

Miriam feeds from Sarah before the mortal woman even realises what is happening, and we see Sarah also apparently taking some of Miriam's blood in return. When Sarah later angrily confronts Miriam and demands an explanation about what is happening to her – a scene which ought to win awards for the most furiously sensual depiction of cigarette smoking ever committed to celluloid – Miriam claims to have given her what she would never have dared to dream of – everlasting life. We, the viewers, know that Miriam isn't quite as generous as she is claiming to be, but when tempted by a vampire as ethereally beautiful as Catherine Deneuve – well, that would be quite the difficult offer to pass up.

One could argue that the scene is still primarily aimed at the male gaze, but this holds less weight when the characters are as strongly written and acted as both Miriam and Sarah undoubtedly are. It's an inescapable fact that the sheer weight of including a sex scene between two such renowned, capable and undeniably beautiful actors does put the rest of the movie rather in the shade. But it's still an essential scene which shows just how women can be as animalistically seductive and deadly as any man.

Not all attempts to bring vampiric sexuality to the screen work quite so well. *Razor Blade Smile* (1998) is a British film that appears to be unsure as to whether it's a straightforward vampire movie or just an hour or so of leather-clad soft porn. Eileen Daly plays vampiric hit-woman Lilith Silver, who hunts her prey in between endless shots of her flicking her hair and baring her fangs in what is clearly supposed to be a seductive manner. It has the effect of making *Razor Blade Smile* possibly the least sexy vampire movie ever, but what it lacks in eroticism it more than makes up for with unintentional humour. The opening scenes of the nineteenth-century duel that end in the death of Lilith's lover and her ensuing transformation into an undead killer are acted out so slowly that on first viewing, one expects it to turn into a comedy skit.

But no. The story, what there is of it, is played straight until the very end, terrible accents and all. The costume designer clearly had an account with a warehouse looking to offload end of line latex catsuits and the camera operator sometimes seems to be following different instructions to the rest of the crew. The end result is a movie that looks like something made by high school drama students for an end of term project, but it's this very naivety that makes *Razor Blade Smile* worth hunting out.

# Chapter Seven

# The Vampire Next Door

Many fictional vampires exist in the 'real' world; ie, a world that is recognisably our own. Adam and Eve in *Only Lovers Left Alive* are so real in their slow and decadent decline that it hurts. Adam's rock star reclusion only perpetuates his myth and makes him more sought out by his fans, in the way that happens endlessly to this day. Clara and Eleanor in *Byzantium*'s bleak British seaside setting are as real as the discarded chip wrappers on the promenade on which they prowl. Betsy Taylor, John Mitchell, even the irritatingly good-looking Cullens from the *The Twilight Saga* – they all have reality in common. They're all attempting to fit into and around 'normal' human life without being discovered – some more successfully than others.

Perhaps that's the precise reason these characters are so popular – we can imagine them existing around us, living next door, possibly being our own next love interest. In *The Radleys* by Matt Haig (Canongate Books, 2010), a family of vampires are hiding in plain sight, disguised by nothing more than a heavy layer of purest beige banality. Peter and Helen Radley are the epitome of a middle-class family – he a family doctor, she an artist – who live with their teenage children in a quiet Yorkshire village. But when their daughter Clara accidentally murders a classmate who sexually assaults her, she realises that she perhaps isn't entirely 'normal' – and the entire family are suddenly at risk of discovery.

The difference in Haig's interpretation of the vampire myth is that his bloodsuckers aren't animals – they're addicts. The Radleys can live without blood if necessary. But it's in the same way that heroin addicts 'could' manage without the gear, or an alcoholic 'could' manage without that second bottle of whisky of an evening – it might be physically possible but the mental strain is another matter entirely. In order to both save Clara from repercussions and to keep the family's true nature secret, Peter and Helen have to confront some uncomfortable truths in their quest to find stability and safety for themselves and their children within a human world that doesn't quite want them but doesn't really know why. Horror and pathos mix to a perfect suburban pitch, as the Radley's fear of losing their human stability becomes as strong as their desire for blood. Their determination to avoid the reality of what they truly are is their eventual downfall, leaving them with no option but to scrape together a patchwork existence as a kind of human-vampire hybrid.

Despite its sometimes bleak tone, *The Radleys* is a joyously uplifting story of people who have never quite fitted in, however hard they try. But does 'fitting in' really suit them anyway? As the all-too-human cracks appear in their lives, we as readers realise – ahead of the characters' own epiphanies – that they will never find real happiness while they are denying their true selves. Emotional betrayals crash down around the Radleys alongside the endless risk of death and destruction. But at the heart of it all is a family who, even if they don't always like each other, are eternally devoted and entwined.

'You're a shark. Be a shark.'

Herrick to John Mitchell,
Being Human, S1E1.

A different take on what it means to be a family is explored in *Being Human*. As with *The Radleys*, Mitchell's blood-drinking is seen more as an addiction than an immoral indulgence. Having spent much of his (after) life killing people, Mitchell is attempting to reclaim his humanity, the success of which ebbs and flows as the trio's story progresses. He clings to his newfound friends as his link to humanity, despite both of them being as paranormal as he is. Together, they learn how to 'be human'.

The full weight of the sheer banal normality of addiction is brought to bear in the series' portrayal of Mitchell as someone who wants to be 'good', but struggles to fight the animal instinct running through his vampire blood. There's a constant raging battle going on between right and wrong, as Mitchell does his utmost to keep on the right side of his own, still very human, moral boundaries. Is there any point to his constant inner turmoil? Should he give in to the beast within and simply enjoy his afterlife to the fullest, not caring about mere mortals that might have the misfortune to get in the way and die as a consequence? It certainly seems the easier option to many around him. When he prevents fellow vampire Seth feeding from patients at the hospital in which he works, Seth gives Mitchell some not so friendly advice. 'Remember that student, the guy … when was it, fifty-eight? Fifty-nine? Or you and Herrick and that girl in the hotel. Or the couple, in the park. You can't stop, Mitchell. It's what we are.' (*Being Human*, S1E1.)

Lauren is a young woman turned by Mitchell at the very beginning of the story. She is bubbly, fun-loving and bouncy and this doesn't change after her death and rebirth – but now she has an edge of panicked malice about her. Lauren carries an inner fear of what she has become that makes her jump into her new and unexpected world recklessly and without care for anyone, including herself. It would be easy to see Lauren as a 'bad guy', if it wasn't for the fact that we know how badly she was treated by Mitchell himself. Having bitten her in the throes of passion during a one night stand that went very, very wrong, Mitchell leaves Lauren to 'wake up' surrounded by strangers. She says, 'It should have been you,' and he knows she's right – he has let her down on all levels, and this becomes yet another stick for him to beat himself with. Mitchell's character is fleshed out further by the depth of his attachment to Herrick, the vampire who made him back on the battlefield. The difference in phrasing is interesting – whereas Herrick 'made' Mitchell, Lauren says 'you took me' – a description that implies brutal sexuality, rather than a considered act. Despite his surface hatred of Herrick and all that he stands for, Mitchell can't quite bring himself to leave his 'maker' in his time of need, resulting in him keeping a deranged Herrick in the loft like a particularly troublesome (and murderous) pet.

Mitchell believes himself to be on the side of good, while also committing evil acts of his own; a walking illustration of the dichotomy that no doubt runs through the psyche of many truly evil, living people. Is Mitchell more acceptable simply because he is classically handsome and wears an air of tragedy lightly around his beautiful physical presentation? We're encouraged to see him as a fallen angel, a Lucifer walking on the earth. As happens so many times in vampire stories, beauty negates inherent evil – we love a truly 'bad' character, but only if they're good looking.

A far glossier version of 'the vampires next door' trope was portrayed in Joel Schumacher's 1987 film *The Lost Boys*. Taking his title from J.M. Barrie's *Peter Pan*, Schumacher uses a familiar storyline – new kids move to town, try to fit in, lock horns with the dodgy locals, end up changing everything – alongside lashings of lip gloss and endless bouffant hairstyles (and that's just the men). The vampires of Santa Carla are dangerously, glamorously tempting; the cool kids on the block who like to look as though they're in charge but who in reality are the true outsiders. They're the epitome of doomed romantic glamour with a rock'n'roll twist, their lair even having a giant poster of Jim Morrison of The Doors on the wall. The Lizard King stands guard over them as they play at being grown ups while never growing older.

Michael is the elder of the two brothers who have just moved into town with their newly divorced mother and, as such, believes himself to be the coolest kid in the family. It isn't long before he has his head turned by Sky, the beautiful consort of local gang leader David. This immediately turns Michael into David's sworn frenemy, laying the foundations for a love story no different to thousands before it. But in order to win the day in this love triangle, Michael really is going to have to fight to the (literal) death. David isn't going to give Sky up lightly, and certainly not to a mere mortal. Michael is goaded into competing for Sky's affections, leaving younger brother Sam to figure out what's really going on – and what's going on is that their new hometown is infested with vampires.

*The Lost Boys* is a movie definitively of its time – the hair styles and dodgy clothes are characters in themselves – but it pulls it off by simply diving fangs first into youth culture and not caring about how it might look as it ages. The soundtrack is clever, including a notable cover of The Doors' 'People Are Strange' by Echo and the Bunnymen. Rather than playing true to the Morrison influence, Schumacher diverts down Uncanny Valley by showing the face of the Sixties' American rock god looking down from a poster while his lyrics are being sung in the 1980s by a vocalist from Liverpool. The film itself subverts the 'glamorous teen movie' that was so popular in the 1980s, parking itself firmly in the 'outsiders' corner so beloved of the goths who made up one of the biggest subcultures at the time. *The Lost Boys* was a gloriously dark and gloomy, out and proud gothic V-sign to the shiny shoes and glossy hairstyles that dominated teen movies of the era.

Vampires, as we know, exist at all levels of society. And can there be anything more attractive than a handsome, well bred *and* intelligent vampire? Matthew Clairmont is all of these things in *A Discovery of Witches*, by Deborah Harkness – a combination that proves irresistible to the reluctant witch, Diana Bishop. The unlikely couple may live in a world in which the supernatural is all too real – and often dangerous –

but like so many before them, the main problem in their lives is the unwillingness of others to accept their love for each other.

One can only imagine how difficult it must be for a human to have a romantic partner who is more than a thousand years old – that's a long time in which to develop annoying habits, by anyone's standards. Their burgeoning relationship isn't helped at the start by Diana's insistence that she does not want to accept the magical side of her life. But blood will out, as it always does, and Diana proves herself to be Matthew's equal, even if others struggle to accept that.

*A Discovery of Witches* is an interesting reinterpretation of the 'vampire = bad guy' trope. Matthew Clairmont is as cultured as can be, while still holding on to his animal instincts. Despite the modern-day setting, the world Diana and Matthew inhabit is still notably rarefied – most readers will start the series knowing nothing about life in the cloistered atmosphere of Oxford University's ancient buildings. It is, in effect, a fantasy novel based around real world locations, which boils down to 'privileged white woman discovers even more privilege and picks up a glamorous – and uber-privileged – boyfriend along the way.' This is taken even further in the subsequent books, as Diana time travels her way (courtesy of Matthew's magical abilities) through the centuries, meeting endless people of note as she goes. Of course, Diana also needs to find someone to help her learn to control her magic – there's nothing society likes less than a woman who isn't under control.

Christopher 'Kit' Marlowe makes an appearance in book two of the series, *Shadow of Night*. Kit Marlowe likes turning up in vampire mythology – one can only assume that he looks a shady sort, too tempting for fiction authors to leave alone. It's not difficult to see why – Marlowe was clearly possessed of both a brilliant mind and a sharp wit, which may well have been put to good use when he allegedly worked as a spy for Queen Elizabeth I during the latter part of the sixteenth century. Interestingly, Harkness portrays Marlowe as a daemon rather than a vampire, pitting him against Diana for Matthew's affection. And the lovelorn world continues to turn, heartbreak and betraying being much the same in the 1600s as in the twenty-first century.

## Monsters in the Media

There is an eternal desire hidden deep within many of us that longs for the vampire to be real. We conveniently forget the icky, murdery side and concentrate on the glamour. Endless life, endless love and, often, endless money. Most of the time we know that it can't and won't happen – we accept that vampires are a myth, albeit one of most enduring myths there is. But we just can't help ourselves – at the first sign of potential proof of vampiric existence, we think, 'but maybe … just maybe'. Hope springs eternal, when one is considering eternity.

Sometimes there is 'proof' that helps prop up such beliefs – but often, that proof is merely our modern gothically-minded imaginations casting a dark shadow over things that are far more mundane, if no less creepy.

The myth of 'vampire graves' has lurked in the darkness for generations. Known as 'mortsafes', they exist in many churchyards – those plots with iron cages above them, often thought to have been built to prevent the undead resident clambering out to chase the townsfolk. Still quite easily found if you know where to look, such graves usually date back to the nineteenth century. There is a good reason for this – rather than being there for our safety in the event of an uprising of the undead, the cages were in fact installed to protect those buried beneath.

Such ironwork was intended to protect the newly interred, in the days when it wasn't unheard of for a buried body to be dug up to see if it wore anything of value. There was also the temptation to steal the body itself and sell it to a local teaching hospital who might ignore provenance in return for acquiring a guinea pig for its students.

Was a young mother *really* threatened by a vampire in her Liverpool home? According to local legend, that's precisely what happened to a woman who was living with her baby in a bedsit in Lodge Lane, Toxteth, in February 1983. Variants on the story can be found, but they all focus on a terrified young girl and her suspicious neighbours. Whatever version of the story you read, it is invariably big on hyperbole. Nothing specifically threatening had ever occurred, but the woman had become so disturbed by the constant feeling of being watched by invisible entities in her apartment. Eventually, hysterical with fear, she had presented herself sobbing at the local police station and begged for help. Claiming that the flat next door to her own 'radiated evilness', the woman was, we are told, promised that police would check the property out in order to reassure her.

Of course, her fears were confirmed – when police broke into the supposedly empty flat, it's said that they found evidence of 'occult practices' having been carried out in the property. If accounts of the time are to be believed, the walls had been painted black and covered with occult symbols, and there was an empty coffin lying in the middle of the floor. If this wasn't enough in itself to scare the living daylights out of anyone, a milk bottle was found near to the coffin that appeared to contain clotted human blood. Despite the property being empty and the erstwhile tenant showing no sign of returning, the poor terrified neighbour scooped up her baby and escaped the city, moving in with relatives safely across the Mersey on the Wirral.

Urban myth? Almost certainly – the story is most often credited to a local author who specialises in paranormal tales of Merseyside. But based, in part at least, on truth? Possibly. The morbid decor could easily be explained away by having been installed by someone with gothic tastes, which was quite fashionable in Britain during the early eighties. Many of us would feel slightly paranoid if we were living alone in what was then quite a tough area, especially as a single mother.

Liverpool has more vampire stories than most, to the point where one could assume there is no smoke without fire – perhaps something really is going on in the underbelly of the bustling port city. But is the city really cursed by the undead, or could the truth perhaps be rather more prosaic? The stories passed down through generations might, in reality, be connected more with public suspicion of the seemingly endless array of immigrants who arrived through the busy docks during the nineteenth and twentieth centuries. Vampirism has often been used as a metaphor for outsiders and intruders; those who we find fascinating while also regarding with suspicion.

Port cities often have a more lax and easy-going approach to those who don't quite fit in. They are also places in which the unusual quickly becomes commonplace. Legends and superstitions arrive on each new cargo ship, carried in by crew from different countries and cultures. Different social and ethnic groups have opinions and habits that don't always sit well with the opinions and habits of others and sooner or later, someone is going to become the bogeyman. Toxteth has always been a multicultural area, populated by those who, for economic or social reasons couldn't or wouldn't live in the more affluent parts of the city. However tolerant and accepting a city might be, there is always going to be a point at which someone needs a scapegoat.

Ann 'Nan' Train lived at 14 Wood Grove, Old Swan. Long demolished, the site of Train's home is now covered by a cul-de-sac just off Edge

Lane. In 1866, Train lived at the property with her mostly absent husband Thomas (a ship's purser whose job meant that he was regularly away from home for periods of time), her maid, 20-year-old Margaret Golding and a lodger, John Thomas Moss. A cousin of Mrs Train, Moss had lodged with the family for some time, despite not being easy company. A notorious womaniser, Moss was also vehemently anti-religion in an age when such opinions were not commonly aired in public. Some swore to have seen his eyes 'light up like burning coals' when he heard mention of Jesus Christ and – glowing eyeballs or not – he was clearly a man who mixed strong opinions with a murky past. It was said that Moss had lived in Australia for some years before returning to Liverpool, but that on his return, his personality had been noticeably changed for the worse. There were whispers of him having attempted suicide by throwing himself from the Albert Dock, only to be dragged from the cold waters of the Mersey by watchmen. He was revived by moonlight, traditionally thought to be a harbinger of spooky things to come.

According to Golding's later witness statements to the coroner's court, Moss wanted a ring that Nan Train had in her possession. Whether he planned to sell it or simply give it to one of his many admirers isn't known, but became aggressive at Train's refusal to hand the jewellery over. When Golding left the room, Moss attacked his cousin, caving in her head with a hatchet. He then ran down the stairs into the scullery and slit his own throat with a knife.

Moss's potential vampire status was helped along by a statement by one Lancaster Harbord, a neighbour of the Trains at their previous address in Bootle. 'I have heard that Moss made the remark that he did not believe in heaven, hell or church, and that he would never go to church unless he was carried there a corpse.' Harbord had previously described Moss as a temperate and intelligent man who rarely drank, which made his sudden murderous rampage all the more unexpected. According to the *Liverpool Echo*, Moss's suicide led to him being buried in unconsecrated ground near to St Anne's Church in the Stanley area of the city.

Across the city in the district of Anfield lies a rather more glamorous creature of the Liverpudlian night. The dual catacombs of Anfield Cemetery have been crumbling for years, their ruined beauty now being frantically salvaged by a team of dedicated volunteers. Somewhere in the underground vaults lie the remains of a Russian noblewoman, interred there after she died while visiting Britain with her husband. Her corpse is, of course, apparently bedecked in the finest jewels, because stories such as this only work if they are overlaid with a veneer of glamorous riches. As far as anyone can ascertain, the basic details of the story are true. A Russian couple were visiting the city when the woman became ill and died. After interring her in the vaults for safekeeping, her bereaved husband returned to Russia, promising that he would be back in due course to build an impressive church in her memory over the spot in which she lay. He failed to return and rumour has it that he remarried, conveniently forgetting his romantic promise.

And there the story would end, if it wasn't for the stories that began springing up during the Second World War. Liverpool lived through its own Blitz from August 1940 until January 1942. Its proximity to the Mersey made it especially vulnerable, not only because its docks were a prime target for the Luftwaffe, but also because the long stretch of water was in itself difficult to keep secure. The entire country was, at the time, dependent on supplies being brought in through the Mersey port and tensions were high. Rumours would regularly travel like wildfire about German submarines being spotted lurking in the depths of the river, and the entire population was on high alert for aerial bombardments. No wonder that there were, on occasion, rather more unusual sightings in the night sky.

People spoke of flying creatures with glowing eyes, that swooped on the unwary. These looked 'foreign', of course – this was an era in which no one was to be trusted and anyone who didn't look recognisably local could be an enemy infiltrator (even in a city with as diverse an ethnic population as Liverpool). The vast majority of damage to the city – as with that in London, Coventry, et al – was inflicted by the distant droning bomber planes that flew over with depressing regularity, but facts were irrelevant in the face of fear. Both the old soldiers standing guard and the terrified families hunkered down in their homes needed a rather more dramatic and more personal enemy with which to contend.

Rumours are just that – rumours. Stories made up (often long after the fact) based on the tiniest nuggets of truth, that are embellished until they serve their true purpose as a more exotic distraction from the mind-numbing horror that was actually going on. Perhaps someone saw flying burning debris one night and briefly mentioned to a companion that it looked like glowing eyes – or perhaps none of it ever happened and the story was made up years later, simply as spooky entertainment. But locals still tell of how they were warned to watch out for the vampires while growing up in the city. And there are still rumours about the bejewelled Russian gentlewoman hidden away among the decaying tombs of Anfield.

On Friday 1 October 1954, Mrs Alice Cullen (not the same Alice Cullen who appears in Twilight, which is rather disappointing for any vampiric conspiracy theorists), then MP for the Glasgow constituency of Gorbals, was quoted in the *Aberdeen Evening Express* as having asked Home Secretary Sir David Maxwell Fyfe to introduce legislation banning the sale of horror comics in the United Kingdom. Her concerns about such publications had been stirred by an incident the previous week, in which Glasgow's Southern Necropolis had been overrun by vampire hunters.

An unusual request in itself, but made all the more so by the fact that the supernatural detectives were all young schoolchildren – and there were hundreds of them. Rumours had spread locally about a 'vampire with iron teeth' that had killed two local children and was apparently still on the look out for more victims. There had been no reports of child murders or disappearances that year, but mere facts didn't deter the determined hunters. On the night of Thursday 23 September, the stories swelled to the point that children began to gather at the Necropolis, many armed with stakes and knives. Some had even brought dogs with them. Police attempting to clear the scene were overwhelmed by the sheer numbers of children running around what was then an unkempt and dilapidated cemetery containing the best part of a quarter of a million graves.

The story made the front page of the *Daily Mirror* on 25 September 1954, which went with the headline, 'AMAZING SCENE AS HUNDREDS OF CHILDREN STORM A CEMETERY'. The sub-header, 'The Toddlers Joined In' shows just how far the excitement had spread among local children. The author of the article clearly had no time for such fairy stories, describing it as a 'stupid tale' while also managing to add his own level of drama to proceedings:

> I walked through the cemetery as darkness was falling. Little boys and girls clung to my coat and shouted: 'Have you come to shoot him, Mister? Kill him, so we can sleep tonight!'
>
> *Daily Mirror*, Saturday 25 September 1954

Having been picked up by the national press, the story developed a life of its own – and blame was laid squarely at the door of imported horror comic books. Dr H.S. Mackintosh, Glasgow's Education Officer, was quoted as saying, 'The horror comics have now gone beyond the bound of license. I hope the Government will take active steps in this very real problem.' Local mothers apparently held similar concerns. 'All the children around here read those horror comics. Last night my seven-year-old son ran home sobbing and pleaded with me to close every window. If we didn't, he said, "the vampire will get us."'

The *Daily Mirror* knew an attention-grabbing topic when they saw one. By Monday 27 September, the story may have been demoted to page three, but the newspaper was now mooting the idea of banning the comics entirely. 'City may ask: Ban the horror comics' they proclaimed, following up with, '[...] civic and welfare leaders in Glasgow—where the 'hunt' took place—have been discussing the incident. They believe American horror comics are to blame for the hysteria and a move may be made to have these types of comics banned.'

On Friday 1 October, the newspaper ramped up public fear even further, with reporter David Craig proclaiming, 'Horror comic hysteria struck again here tonight,' after a family of travellers were attacked in their caravan by children throwing stones and shouting that the occupants were witches. The mother of the family was quoted as saying, 'The children were whooping like Indians, and at one point there must have been at least 300 of them in the field.' Nearby resident Mrs Agnes McLean added, 'The place was black with children and traffic was held up while they surged across the road. People around here blame these dreadful comics of which there is so much talk just now.'

Ironically, it is likely that the story of the Gorbals Vampire hadn't sprung from imported comics after all, but rather came from a traditional story that began life far closer to home. The Necropolis backed onto an ironworks that was known locally as Dixon's Blazes and which regularly lit up the night sky with the roaring glow of the furnaces. One of the boys present on that famous vampire-hunting night told the BBC, 'The red light and the smoke would flare up and make all the gravestones leap. You could see figures walking about at the back all lined in red light.'

As a background for a looming 'city of the dead' it would have been hard to beat for sheer gothic creepiness. Added to this was the poem 'Jenny Wi' the Iron Teeth', written by Alexander Anderson in 1879, which at the time was on the curriculum in Scottish primary schools. Most of the children out hunting the monster would have been familiar with lines such as:

> Mercy me, she's at the door,
> Hear her lift the sneck;
> Whisht! an' cuddle mammy noo
> Closer roun' the neck.

Regardless of the original source for the legend, the national media was now demanding that the powers-that-be do something about the craze that had gripped so many children. A memo, marked 'SECRET' and sent jointly from the Secretary of State to the Home Office, Secretary of State for Scotland and Minister for Education on 25 November 1954 spoke of the complications that would come from banning an entire genre of comics – in short, there was no legal definition of what constituted 'obscene'. Under the Obscene Publications Act 1857, 'obscene' was generally accepted to apply only to publications that were graphically sexual in nature. This doesn't mean that the Secretary of State was on the side of the comic books:

> These objectionable comics are not obscene within the meaning of the existing law, but they are just as harmful, if not more harmful to children and young persons as publications which are obscene, and the courts ought to be given the same power to prevent their circulation as they have to prevent the circulation of obscene publications.

Prime Minister Winston Churchill was sent samples of such supposedly offensive publications – an innocent collection to modern eyes, full of stories of cowboys and private detectives, Frankenstein and (unbelievably) Captain Marvel. One can only imagine what the elder statesman made of such a collection. Regardless, the comic books had been deemed 'unsuitable' and they had to go.

The Children and Young Persons (Harmful Publications) Act 1955 was introduced by Home Secretary Gwilym Lloyd George in May 1955 and came into force on 6 June. It was prompted almost entirely by the drama of the Gorbals Vampire incident and applied to:

> any book, magazine or other like work which is of a kind likely to fall into the hands of children or young persons and consists

wholly or mainly of stories told in pictures (with or without the addition of written matter), being stories portraying–(a) the commission of crimes; or (b) acts of violence or cruelty; or (c) incidents of a repulsive or horrible nature; in such a way that the work as a whole would tend to corrupt a child or young person into whose hands it might fall.

Despite the vagueness of its last sentence, it is still in force today; perhaps *because* of said vagueness, there have been barely any prosecutions brought through it.

Even before the Gorbals vampire brought fear to the parents and politicians of the United Kingdom, comic books were being vilified in the United States. In November 1953, Fredric Wertham MD wrote an article for *Ladies Home Journal* magazine, titled 'What Parents Don't Know About Comic Books.' In it, the good doctor asserted that:

Juvenile delinquency has increased about 20 per cent since 1947. It is, however, not the number but the kind of delinquency that is the salient point. Younger and younger children commit more and more serious and violent acts. Even psychotic children did not act like this fifteen years ago.

[…] There is nothing in these 'juvenile delinquencies' that is not described in comic books. […] In comic books usually these crimes remain unpunished until the criminal has committed many more of them. Children are not so lucky. They face severe punishments whenever they are caught. Educated on comic books, they go on to a lone postgraduate course in jails (with the same reading matter).

Perhaps surprisingly, up until his public battle against horror comics, Wertham had developed a reputation for being a forward-thinking psychiatrist. In an era of segregation and bigotry, Wertham treated black patients at his mental health clinic in Harlem, New York, and was often cited in court cases concerning segregation issues. Regardless of his liberalism in some areas, Wertham was clear in his belief that horror comics were the root cause of many cases of juvenile delinquency in children and young adults. In a classic case of mistakenly believing that correlation equals causation, Wertham stated that 95 per cent of children in reform schools read horror comics, *ergo*, horror comics taught children to be criminals.

Wertham was called to give expert testimony to an enquiry run by the newly formed Senate Subcommittee on Juvenile Delinquency. Although the final report into investigation didn't wholly blame comics for the supposed rise in the youth crime rates, a recommendation was made that the industry took more responsibility for its content. This led to the foundation of the Comics Code Authority, which required publishers to restrict the use of certain images and words. Given the rather arbitrary restrictions – the word *zombie* was one singled out for censorship, as were *crime* and *terror* – and the Code's insistence that all stories should end with any criminals being suitably punished, comic books rapidly became more sanitised and relied on 'super hero' characters, rather than anything that could be translated into 'real life'.

Comic books have continued to be blamed for all manner of incidents and prosecutions for publishing 'obscene' comics still happen. In 1994, a comic book artist by the name of Mike Diana became the first person to be convicted of 'artistic obscenity', for writing and publishing his comic series *Boiled Angel*. Word of his arrest had spread quickly through the comic book industry and his case was taken up by the Comic Book Legal Defense Fund, which had been set up in 1986 to fight censorship in comic books on the grounds of free speech. The CBLDF lost the case – Diana was fined and sentenced to three years probation, a condition of which was to not draw any cartoons – but they continue to fight against censorship in cartoons to this day.

Highgate Cemetery sits on a charmingly beautiful and peaceful spot on Highgate Hill in north London, its quiet cloisters and air of being, at heart, a country park somewhat at odds with the knowledge that tens of thousands of bodies are buried within its boundaries. Divided into two plots – East and West – by Swains Lane cutting through its middle, Highgate is the home of many of the great and the good, whose only common ground is that they are dead.

The West Cemetery is the older of the two sections, many of its tombs still showing critical signs of ageing despite the ongoing care and attention given by the many members of staff and volunteers who view Highgate as a beloved friend. Its rather gothic decline in the 1970s made it the perfect setting for films such as *Taste The Blood of Dracula*, starring Christopher Lee. In February 1970, David Farrant of Muswell Hill wrote to the Hampstead and Highgate Express about his theory that a supernatural being was roaming the old cemetery at night. He had, he said, on three separate occasions witnessed a grey, 'ghost-like' figure through the gates on Swains Lane, apparently wandering around the graves. Other readers got in touch with the newspaper with their own ghostly sightings, including some asserting that the 'being' floated and had glowing red eyes.

Self proclaimed 'vampire hunter' Sean Manchester had his own opinions about Highgate Cemetery and he wasn't afraid to share them with the public. Described as the 'president of the British Occult Society', Manchester told the press that he believed the apparition to be an Eastern European vampire, which he intended to publicly exorcise. The media lapped up the spooky drama and reported on Manchester's claims with front page headlines such as 'Does a wampyr walk in Highgate?' (*Hampstead and Highgate Express*, Friday 17 February, 1970). The myth of the 'Highgate Vampire' began to take hold.

The change of description from ghost to possible vampire drew widespread attention, from which neither Farrant nor Manchester shied away. Manchester was interviewed for ITV's nationally broadcast *Today* programme on Friday 13 March 1970 and claimed that he planned to exorcise the Highgate vampire later that same night. Public interest was such that hundreds of fellow would-be vampire hunters climbed the walls of the dilapidated cemetery and swarmed the grounds while police attempted to restore order.

With hindsight, it is easy to see that much of the myth was created by Manchester himself, who spun the thinnest of stories out into an exponentially larger mythology, the media interest spawned a longstanding urban myth. The two men developed a bitter rivalry over the years, once declaring that they were to take part in a 'magician's duel' on Parliament Hill on Friday 13 April 1973 (it never happened). Despite being the more reticent of the pair, Farrant didn't hold back in his open dislike of his rival. He wrote a satirical comic strip, *The Adventures of Bishop Bonkers*, in which he portrayed Manchester as a paranoid maniac whose evil plans were foiled by, of course, Farrant himself. In 2011, Farrant went so far as to film himself raising a toast to an effigy of Manchester's head, which was presented with great ceremony on a silver platter.

This rivalry, which lasted until Farrant's death in 2019, was mainly due to the differences in their interpretation of the Highgate myth. Farrant generally kept to describing the supposed entity as a ghost or spirit, whereas Manchester insisted fervently that it was, unquestionably, a vampire.

# Chapter Eight

# The Enduring Glamour of the Gothic

'From beginning to end. Death completes you.'

(*Dracula*, 2020. BBC – Gatiss & Moffat)

There seems to be no end to our insatiable thirst for bloody anti-heroes (and heroines), along with the fashions and decor that goes with it. 'Goth' is to this day one of the most popular subcultures in both music and fashion, with Victorian mourning-wear still being the dress code of choice for a huge amount of people around the world. We now live in a world where you can buy (surprisingly realistic) fake fangs on Amazon along with your skull ornaments and spiderweb earrings

The goth subculture climbed out of the grave and into the daylight in early 1980s' Britain, during an era of political unrest and economic depression. Spawned from post-punk clubs in northern England, it began its (after)life as a new genre of music but rapidly developed into a fully formed culture all of its own. Unlike most trends in music and fashion, goth is – quite aptly – the love that never dies.

One could argue for days about who and what should be classed as goth – even the most notable goth musicians themselves disagree about it in many cases. The term 'gothic rock' wasn't even new. As far as can be established it was originally used by John Stickney in 1967, writing in college newspaper *The Williams Record* about Jim Morrison and The Doors. The Lizard King really did deserve his place on the cave wall in *The Lost Boys*. Music is as vital to many people as breathing and endless musicians have channelled their love of the undead into their work.

Probably the first thing anyone will come up with when challenged to name a song about vampires is *Bela Lugosi's Dead* by Bauhaus. Once described by lead singer Peter Murphy as 'the Stairway To Heaven of the 1980s', it became even more embedded in gothic mythology when it was used in *The Hunger*. Written by guitarist Daniel Ash and bass player David J, the lyrics to *Bela* were inspired by old horror films that David J had been watching on television in the late 1970s. The song is an oddity from the start, based on a bossa nova beat with a riff that Ash later realised had been inspired by, of all things, an old Gary Glitter song. Engineered by Derek Tompkins at Beck Studios in Wellingborough, Northamptonshire, *Bela* was not only recorded in one take, it was the first time Bauhaus had stepped foot into a professional studio. When Murphy's vocal finally comes in – more than two-and-a-half minutes into the song – we're hearing the first ever recording of him singing into a studio microphone (he also had a cold at the time, which only adds to the intense sound of the vocals). The song is perhaps something of a millstone round the necks of Bauhaus themselves, who have on occasion tried to distance themselves from the 'goth' tag (without much success). It's easy to forget that they have a huge body of other work that doesn't mention so much as a single fang. But *Bela Lugosi's Dead* is still the song that instantly evokes the spirit of the vampire in many people.

'Horror-country' is a niche market by any standards, but it's hard to deny the unexpected jollity of *Return of the Vampire* by Swedish band The Coffinshakers (2007). Sounding like the undead Johnny Cash, vocalist Rob Coffinshaker (a wonderful name, but actually born Robert Fjällsby) tells straightforward tales of traditional blood suckers to a toe-tapping country beat. With their other songs including titles such as *Dracula Has Risen From The Grave* (after the 1968 Hammer Films production of the same name, starring Christopher Lee). Complete with Spinal Tap-esque back stories – their original drummer apparently left 'to study voodoo practices' – The Coffinshakers prove that you don't have to be dour to be undead.

Occasionally a song that's intended to be satire is misinterpreted as a serious comment, as happened with 1981's *Release The Bats* by The Birthday Party. Despite often appearing in curated lists of 'best goth tracks ever', it was only ever intended to be a self-parody, playing on the press's determination to pigeonhole the band into the newly emerging goth scene. Written by Mick Harvey and Nick Cave, the song is a cacophony of noise over a thudding beat, with lyrics mostly made up of random vampire-related words, mocking the band's unwanted status as the gothic gods du jour. Musicians are the perfect addition to vampire movies, whether or not they themselves are bloodsuckers. Adam in *Only Lovers Left Alive* is the epitome of the louche, nihilistic muso who is adored by many but is, in private, world-weary and sick of his own public image. In *Queen of the Damned*, Lestat is literally dragged back into the living world by the pull of rock music.

The lure of the darker side of life is one that is as strong today as it has ever been. Social media has made it even easier to join forces with likeminded children of the night, even if it's just to discuss how best to decorate a baby's nursery in shades of black (the answer is always 'add some black and white stripes' – the influence of Tim Burton's *The Nightmare Before Christmas* is strong in gothic home decor). Want an authentic Victorian cinching corset? The internet now provides instructions on how to make one yourself, or you can have a replica shipped from China at a very reasonable price in less time than it took Dracula to travel from the Carpathians to Whitby. The specifics of the lifestyle might change slightly – steampunk took centre stage for a while, but eventually settled back down and allowed black taffeta and thick eyeliner to retake its place on the Goth Throne – but eventually it all comes back to the same three things – sex, death and graveyards.

Modern life can be stressful and downright scary, with horror stories being pushed into our faces from the moment we open our eyes and look at the phone waiting patiently beside our bed. Most of us live in relatively modern houses with all essential amenities, a luxury that has given us the breathing space in which to romanticise earlier times. They were times when poverty, abuse and appallingly low standards of health and hygiene laid waste to huge swathes of communities across the globe. Yet in many other ways they were simpler, because when you're constantly battling to survive you don't have time to worry about the smaller trials and tribulations of life.

Those heavy skirts probably had lice in them and the crumbling castle definitely didn't have a central heating system. If you had a husband he might well die of syphilis or be killed in military service and your children's chances of surviving infancy were very low indeed. But you wouldn't have had to worry about whether you'd answered all your emails and there were no targeted ads popping up in front of your eyeballs as you had your first cup of tea of the day, trying to persuade you to buy a discounted frock before you've even had breakfast. No – all you'd have to think about was whether the red velvet skirt looked better than the green and maybe that dilapidated sash window in the bedroom ought to be left open a crack? After all, you'd noticed a bat flapping at the cracked glass in the early hours on a few occasions now and, well, it would be shame not to let it in for a warm wouldn't it?

I spoke to a cross section of people who have been involved in the goth scene one way or another over the years, and asked them what they thought about the ongoing human fascination with all things dark and deadly.

## The Musician

Wayne Hussey is the vocalist and driving force behind The Mission, a band that has been associated with the goth scene since its inception in 1986.

**Seeing Christopher Lee as Dracula in the 1958 Hammer adaptation was the first time a screen vampire stirred something more than fear in me, even if I didn't quite recognise it at the time. Who is your most memorable character from any vampire movie, and why?**
Being a red-blooded young teenage boy with a raging libido it has to be Ingrid Pitt and her ravishing décolletage that fuelled a thousand fantasies. The thought of Ingrid sinking her fangs into my neck as she pulled my head into her bosom, I would've gladly surrendered my human life to her.

**When I was younger my parents clearly hoped that goth was a phase I'd grow out of, but I'm 50 at the time of writing this and the most recent picture I put up in my living room was a framed photo of Sharon Tate from the set of Fearless Vampire Killers. It's clearly a very long-lived 'phase' – something I've noticed with many friends and acquaintances over the years. Why is it do you think that goth appears to be for life, rather than just for Hallowe'en?**
Well, I guess for some, goth is a lifestyle choice that persists. But I do also think there are plenty of tourists too. And that's more than okay by me. It *is* a phase that some go through but for others it touches their soul, it resonates, and informs who and how they are and how they see their place in the world. And we tend to gravitate to others that share our interests, our aesthetics, our lifestyle choices. There's always safety in numbers. I think the human fascination and attraction for the 'darker' side is a constant, some embrace it and some run scared.

**How do you feel about being perceived as a goth icon – is it a millstone or a badge of honour?**

I really don't consider myself as an icon of any kind anymore, although I'm flattered that you think I am. To me goth icons are people like Siouxsie, Robert Smith, & Carl McCoy. Maybe I was a little in the 80s but these days not so. Certainly back then I could look out at our audience and see people who had come to the show dressed as me – with the a big black hat and dark glasses and a love heart painted on their cheeks. And I enjoyed that and was flattered. But, just as it was something that I grew out of so did most of our audience.

**If you were offered the chance of becoming immortal – as you are now, with no further mental or physical deterioration – would you take it (and why)?**

Tempting, but I think not. I would certainly take the option for a few years extra but not forever. I'd have to watch so many loved ones die and my heart would get broken over and over again and I'm not sure I'd want to endure that. Mind you, think of all the books I could read that I've been meaning to read, films to see, music to listen to, places to visit……
Mmmm, yes, tempting. But no thanks.

## The Accidental Goth Activist

Lee Meadows co-founded World Goth Day with his friend Martin Oldgoth in 2009. I asked him how he came to love gothic culture and whether he was surprised that a joke between friends so quickly became a huge cultural event.

*Lee*: I developed an (unhealthy) relationship with the darker aspects of life when I was probably old enough to pay more than fleeting attention to what was on the TV at the time; notably the creepier episodes of *Dr Who, Sapphire and Steel* (if you can remember that), terrible Hammer Horror movies of the 1970s and more significantly, that one time on *Top Of The Pops* in 1979 when Gary Numan's pale, robotic posturing creeped the absolute nonsense out of me when Tubeway Army hit the charts with *Are Friends Electric?* I was scared but boy, was I gripped.

From then on the usual 80s minor-chord oriented pop idol suspects were my musical diet; Duran Duran, Japan, Toyah Wilcox, etc. but the attraction to Goth in general didn't really hit me proper until one Saturday evening when *Alice* by The Sisters Of Mercy started playing out of the radio. I'd heard nothing like it before and I swear, I actually felt the jarring in the back of my head as the 'Goth Mode' switch was finally flicked. From then on the universe seemingly flooded my ears with music by The Mission, All About Eve & Bauhaus via night time radio as though John Peel & Annie Nightingale were on a mission to complete my transformation for a 'bigger plan'. I won't lie, I fully appreciate that at the time I was once thin enough to make black clothes & pointy boots look good, so it wasn't long before the final decorations went on and I somehow 'belonged'.

World Goth Day (or just 'Goth Day' as it was dubbed in its conception) was a caffeine-fuelled epiphany that I had one evening after learning that BBC 6Music were planning to play a full day of music & interviews dedicated to Goth on 22 May 2009. I'd decided that there should be one day a year in which the Gothic community should be able to celebrate its existence. Like a giant Pride festival I suppose, but with bats and big hair. I wrote a hurried and extensive blog on Myspace about the idea and lo & behold, a great big chunk of England took notice and did just that. Goth clothes were worn to the workplace, appropriately spooky music was requested by people on their local radio stations and the ubiquitous 'goth smiley' logo that I'd drawn up in Photoshop was being distributed and shared on people's social media pages or printed out and stuck on the windows of homes and the media slowly took notice.

The following year the decision was made to 'go global' after a conversation with fellow DJ Martin Oldgoth. Between us a World Goth Day website was created, proper social media accounts put in place and a big push to promote the idea made worldwide. 22 May was going to be World Goth Day every year, just because. Big names in the Goth scene were on our side from the off. It was a hugely successful exercise in creating positivity using social media and I'm pleased to say that World Goth Day continues to be as popular now as it was from the beginning. It barely needs any push from me anymore; people actually spend the few months prior to 22 May planning what they're going to do. This is something I'd always wanted from the off – for WGD to have legs of its own and maybe even outlive me.

Each year I dutifully catalogue every single WGD event I'm notified about and update the website accordingly. It always amazes me just how much interest there is in South America and Mexico, who often both outnumber the rest of the globe for WGD events. I literally have no idea why this is. It could be the music, it could be the escape from reality the Goth scene offers which maybe for them, hits home a little harder than life further North. Logistically, the last place I would want to be hanging out with large numbers of people wearing thick black clothes is somewhere densely humid and equatorial, but apparently what do I know?

The Amazon has ACTUAL GOTHS LIVING IN IT. Go on, Google it. The proof is out there and I'm stunned. Elegant youths, dressed in black and showing absolutely no sign of dehydration or at least, not on fire. I've come to befriend a few South American and Mexican Goths and they are the most wonderful people I've ever spent time around.

## The Aesthete

Dr Nadia van der Westhuizen has a PhD in English Literature/Cultural and Critical Studies with a focus on contemporary adaptations of fairy tales and myths in genre fiction, particularly the Gothic. She works at University College London.

**Have you always been interested in dressing 'differently'? Did you fit in with your peers as a child and just develop an individual style as you got older, or have you always stood out from the crowd?**
It's never easy to articulate one's experience of childhood without imposing some measure of adult judgement, but it is safe to say that I have always been alternative to the heteronormative mainstream. I was very introverted as a child, and as I grew up it became increasingly apparent that I was different to most of my peers in terms of my interests and inclinations. That said, I had an incredibly loving and supportive home life, and was always able to make friends, so I never felt isolated or lonely. I was therefore able to develop quickly and easily, and became involved in the goth scene while still very young.

**What attracted you to goth in the first place?**
It just absolutely fit who I was, and what I needed and wanted in my social life. Every aspect of it, from the music and literature to the aesthetics, felt right. From the first, it was a safe space where I could be

completely myself. Thus to me it is not a style that I have adopted but rather a reflection of who I am. I know some consider goth to be a style of music or dress only, but for me and my loved ones it is our culture and it permeates every aspect of our lives. Perhaps most importantly, it has also allowed me to connect with others like me. It is human nature to 'tribe' and it has been a tremendous benefit and blessing to find my tribe so easily.

**Do you have any particular style icons?**
Aesthetically, the female horror icons of the late twentieth century (Vampira, Morticia Addams, Lily Munster, Elvira) and the female music icons which have shaped the goth scene (Siouxsie Sioux, Patricia Morrison) have probably had the greatest influence. I've also always loved B-movies – especially vampire films – and the styling of the female vampires in European cinema (Patty Shepard, Isabelle Adjani, Soledad Miranda), and the many 'brides' of the Hammer Horror Draculas, have left an imprint. However, I feel my style has developed not only from the visual media but in part from the Gothic literature I've read. Not only the Gothic heroines, but the actual descriptions of the complexity of Gothic beauty – haunting and beguiling yet also dark and sometimes sinister – is what has really driven my personal aesthetic.

**You make a lot of your own clothing and accessories – does it take up a huge amount of time and effort? And did you teach yourself, or already have a creative background?**
Creativity was encouraged in my household, so I grew up feeling that it was a normal and necessary part of life to express oneself through art and craft. As a teenager, I even attended an art school that placed as much emphasis on teaching practical creative skills as it did academic subjects. I am therefore quite experienced at making things, yet also very much enjoy experimenting with new processes. As I work to an academic schedule, I become very busy at certain times of the year but there are periods where I am able to be more creative. I believe that it is important to mental and emotional health to have creative outlets, so I always endeavour to indulge my artistic and creative urges – whether it is painting and photography, or jewellery making and sewing – as often as I can.

**You obviously have a very strong and striking image. Is this a 24/7 look, or do you sometimes go out barefaced wearing scraggy leggings and an old jumper?**
Like most, I dress-up for special events but need to be a little more practical in my day-to-day and work attire. However, I would imagine many people would still consider my daily look to be different to the mainstream as I still wear what could be considered to be elaborate makeup and clothing. I never go out barefaced because, like many in the scene, I believe that I am projecting my internal self onto my exterior through makeup and clothing and am therefore not actually being myself until I am wearing my 'true' face. My makeup and clothing are inexorably tied to my identity, and even though they are sometimes more subtle than at other times, they are always necessary.

**Why do you think gothic culture is so important to so many people?**
Anthropologically speaking, culture is a vital part of life that influences everything including our customs, views, beliefs, loyalties, social behaviour, and even our aspirations and fears. It provides important social benefits and enhances quality of life for both individuals and communities. As with any other culture, goth culture enriches lives and connects people to each other. We are a living, thriving community and our culture and its heritage reflects our identity and our integrity as a people. It is important because culture is fundamental to the human experience, and it allows us to live fuller, richer lives.

## The Promoter

Kirstin Lavender is a promoter and band manager from Yorkshire, who also organises the Tomorrow's Ghosts Festival at Whitby, England.

*Kirstin:* I don't actually think it [gothic culture] is particularly important as a moniker in itself – but the impact it has had on music, the arts, film, architecture and literature certainly is. 'Goth' was a term coined by the media to pigeonhole something that wasn't mainstream, but as the decades went by, it became something in its own right and it keeps evolving. I think growing up goth or any other alternative look was just a darker version of everything else that was already out. To me personally, it was only ever about the music and literature. I suppose that depends what you're drawn to.

As a small child with an elder brother who was a New Romantic/ Post Punk lad, I was exposed to bands like Teardrop Explodes, Classix Nouveaux, Japan, Soft Cell and David Bowie. I detested the late 80s high street fashion which was the latter part of school for me – everyone was wearing Joe Bloggs jeans with those hideous patches and was obsessed with Bros. I knew what I didn't like but I didn't think too much about it, I just wore a lot of black!

My father was a huge 'Hammer Horror' fan and would show me films like *Blood From The Mummy's Tomb* and *Dracula*, so I could soon be found floating around gigs and clubs wearing long white Hammeresque dresses with plunging necklines. I loved the female characters and how they dressed. We also used to watch *The Addam's Family* which I never actually enjoyed, (I preferred *The Munsters*). I don't want to come across as a person who's life was filled with nothing but goth because it wasn't – I loved *The Golden Girls* and *The Wonder Years*.

My brother was twelve years older than me, so I would watch him getting ready for his nights out around Leeds, which was a mecca for great live music and nightclubs. He'd have the likes of Marc Almond, David Sylvian and Steve Luigi crash over and I would come downstairs to find these men had set up camp on my favourite spot on the sofa. Later down the line, David was occasionally given babysitting duties on Saturday mornings when my parents were at work. So many little things will have most likely led to me loving the music I do.

A late cousin of mine was a lampy [lighting crew] – he worked on some of the early Sisters Of Mercy gigs in and around London and would also help out doing bits and bats backstage. On a family trip to London, I got to see one of my first ever gigs, the famous Sisters' Royal Albert Hall one. Apparently I managed to annoy Eldritch because there 'was a child backstage eating Wotsits' in their room. See, I was a cool kid!

**Whitby is world renowned for its goth weekenders. What made you want to take on such a big event?**
We went to many a great 'goth weekend' in Whitby but for the last eight years, only went twice. We were, for a short time running 'Absinthe Goth Festival' up at The Met Ballroom and when we were asked to bring our event to the Pavilion we leapt at the chance. A really good working relationship was formed and here we are. Having more space

to accommodate bands meant we could ask bigger bands to play, which broadened the net. We've not kept it strictly goth, but have kept it 'alternative', so to speak.

**You're closely connected to the Stoker family through his great-grand-nephew Dacre. What do you think Bram would have made of the continued adoration of his infamous (anti)hero, more than a century after his creation?**

Bram was a very forward-thinking man of his time who championed women's rights, and was interested in modern technology, which was included in *Dracula*. I think he would wholeheartedly approve of how Dracula has evolved throughout the decades but I reckon he might have thrown the script for *Twilight* into the grave and ordered a carpark to be built over it! The wonderful thing about Dacre is that he has many similarities to Bram in the sense they were both athletes and scholars, and their ability to write great books. There can be a lot of snobbery around the story of Dracula as many people feel certain books, films, series haven't stayed loyal to the original but every time something new has come out, I see Dacre is welcoming of other interpretations of the book and keeping an open mind is what allows the theme to evolve and stay.

**Do you think there will still be a subculture of people who like wearing black and sitting in graveyards a century from now?**

I'm not sure but I really hope so! I also hope some of my descendants will like sleeping in cemeteries drinking red wine, pretending it's blood and wearing black wedding dresses down the local pub because of course, we never did any of this ... ahem! I come from a very long line of Irish Catholic nuns, priests and morticians so I hope my descendants choose to do something more feckin' cheerful with their lives!

# Interview with Jonny Brugh

Jonny Brugh has worked in television and comedy for many years, but is probably best known – in the UK, at least – for playing retired 'Nazi vampire' Deacon Brucke in the 2014 comedy horror, *What We Do In The Shadows*.

I chatted to Jonny about undead style, favourite vampires and the power of erotic dance.

**Are there any funny vampire habits or characteristics that you thought of but didn't get to do in the film?**
Not really. All I had with me was a petulant temperament I had played with seven years earlier, when we made *Interviews With Some Vampires*. Perhaps a general sense of boredom, a desire to just slaughter any guests and the single line, 'send their souls to hell'. Cripes, that seems so awful now! I kept trying to slide it in during scenes but Vladislav would interject and show a surprisingly resourcefulness which played well into the main comedy game, which was 'be dramatic and undermine it with domesticity'. You can see it during a mainly improvised scene in the basement when the cops were searching the house. Deacon suggested they eat the police and Vlad suggests we wait to see what other 'Fire Safety' issues there might be.

This way of writing is my favourite. But you need comic performers who enjoy playing together. It's a good example of how actors only need simple character traits to make a scene work. Often, being too prepped limits possibilities for humour and there was a general note to keep the script hidden from the actors to avoid being preoccupied with too much prep, or we'd miss wonderful confused moments that make a film like *Shadows* funny. Actors can be too rehearsed and they stop listening and playing.

Great filmmakers are the ones who see things on the day, in the moment of play and can adapt on the spot. As long as we know the purpose of the scene so we can play around it. So, for me, on *Shadows*, I just let myself play in the moment and let situations create the character.

**What was your inspiration for the way you interpreted Deacon's character?**

There is no 'interpretation' of Deacon, I invented him and brought him to the shoot. Deacon is me, a version of me, an alter ego that I suppress in real life so as not to offend others. I think we all do this. The writers had no idea and continued to have no idea what I would do. That was the writers' request – 'surprise us'.

I could rephrase the question: *What was the inspiration for choosing Deacon's actions and reactions?* He should be sexy and nerdy, so knitting and erotic dance should do the trick.

I wanted to play a barbarous arsehole. I chose to do this to contrast with what I knew Jemaine and Taika would be doing. Again, we had played the short film before the feature and had a good idea of how they would play it. I also looked forward to playing the awful Alter Ego.

During the shoot we were able to adjust temperament and attitude in our improvisations, based on what the scene and story required. This way the character is built simply by what happens in the scenes and what they are facing, but in an improvised clumsy way. Since the scenes are shot out of order and I was not privy to any script, I paid little attention to character progression or development. In hindsight we can see how 'not worrying about too much detail' can work fine. I think this works for Deacon – the documentary is such a small moment in his looong undead life. As an actor I'm constantly watching to see what writers and directors have in mind, sometimes discovering mid-scene that they had nothing in mind. It brought the best moments out of us.

**Re. Deacon's personal style – do you have a personal affinity with the old vampire movies or was it more a case of dressing him like the clichéd rocker who still thinks he's 20?**

Most of Deacon's fashion came from his history of being a soldier, stealing his uniform or others' uniforms as mementos of his past. Costume designer Amanda Neal sourced a number of uniform jackets. I wanted to have a big furry collar and or animal fur or skin; boots obviously, leather pants and a huge brass belt buckle. There had been discussions before production about how costume informs the characters. I've always enjoyed 'Clown' as a performance. Clown uses costume in wonderful ways to create a whole character – the costume can come first, as can makeup. I got a better instinct for Deacon once I had the pleasure of putting his costume on, spending a few days in it and talk through it.

**Do you enjoy vampire story culture?**

Not so much. I enjoy some kitsch parts of vampire chic and I love *Bram Stoker's Dracula* 'cos Gary Oldman is brilliant. If there was anything I took with me from vampire culture, albeit in a subconscious way, it would be the grumpy bits of Gary Oldman's *Dracula*.

**Was the infamous erotic dance scene improvised?**

The dance was fully improvised so as to bring with it the brutal truth of dance, the bits that are not successful, the bits in-between dance moves.

There was some prep. I knew Deacon was into erotic dance so when we found ourselves idea-less one morning I offered an erotic dance moment. The entire crew sat and waited while the costume department and I had a quick think. I wanted a fishnet vest – yes, we have one right here! Great! Now for some 'Snake Charming Music' with little rhyme and some moves. I had looked at the erotic dance scene in Metropolis so I tried to homage it. All those strange movements are so captivating!

It's not easy to dance like that in front of forty professional filmmakers! Taika, who was behind the camera, would throw out a wiggling leg or an arm to help along. All I knew was that Deacon would give little thought to embarrassment; he was too busy being 'In The Zone' to even consider that it wasn't sexy. There's a message for all of us there ... or is there?

**Which is your own favourite movie/TV vampire?**

*Bram Stoker's Dracula* is the only vamp film I'd put on again. Other than that I like *Shadows* the film and the USA tele series [the television adaptation of *What We Do In The Shadows*]. I like unhinged, other worldly characters but I'm not hugely interested in vampire or Halloween culture.

**If all the legendary vampires were real, which one would you genuinely be afraid of?**

Perhaps the vamps from *30 Days Of Night*. They are so fucked up animalistic and in a really cold, shark-esque way. It's the lack of humanity and empathy that makes it scary. Stick that on a human face – that's scary, akin to *Demons* but colder.

# Interview with Dacre Stoker

**You've led an interesting life in your own right – teaching, athletics, etc. Did you always have it in the back of your mind to take up the guardianship of the family name, or was that something that just naturally fell to you over the years?**

*Dracula* went into public Domain in 1962, long before I got involved in my research and writing about my great-grand-uncle. My interest is primarily to learn as much as I can about Bram Stoker and trying to understand his life, his work and his inspirations for writing.

**Why do you think society is so fascinated by vampires as a species?**

The myth of the Vampire has been around for centuries, some version of a creature returning from the grave haunting or taking life from the living is very deeply rooted in most every culture in the world. In the early eighteenth century people believed in these myths and mistook the effects of contagious diseases to be signs of real vampires. Today we are enlightened to know differently but still the interest in the possibility of immortality is appealing. The fascination in vampires, I believe, revolves around the power and the sexuality that is associated with vampires in literature comics, TV shows, and movies.

**Dracula is generally seen as the overlord of all the 'modern' vampire interpretations, with endless film/books/tv adaptations using Bram Stoker's original story as the jumping off point for their own. Why do you think the Count has turned out to be the most popular vampire of them all?**

Simply because he was based on a real person Vlad Dracula III. The fascination to connect the fictional character to the historical person has raised a lot of profile as well as concern among some Romanians.

I do think that Bram was a genius for using Vlad Dracula III's name for his Vampire Count, not only did Bram connect his fictional Count to a real historical figure, he also used portions of Transylvania, which was geographically adjacent to the province of Walachia, where Vlad Dracula III reigned for 7½ years. This was a part of the world which was mysterious to Bram's readers in 1897, he capitalised on its mysterious nature and it's strange and little-known culture. This combined with real concerns of vampires dating back to the early 1700s in many countries in this region. By combining real places and a plausible central character based on a real historical figure, Bram created a sort of fictional propaganda which was quite convincing. When Bela Lugosi starred on stage as Count Dracula, with his Hungarian accent, and years later films depicted all vampires originating from Transylvania, this pretty much cemented the reputation that some Romanians struggle with and/or benefit from today. Over the last seven years on my tours to Romania I have found that tourism is beginning to focus not only on the fictional Count Dracula but also on the historical Vlad Dracula III, in my opinion this is healthy and a way to 'set the story straight'.

**Which is your favourite film/TV interpretation of Dracula and why?**
I don't have just one, it is too hard to choose mainly because there are so many spread over the past century. Here are my top four, the 1931 *Dracula* by Todd Browning with Bela Lugosi for its originality and novelty. *Horror of Dracula* 1958 with Christopher Lee, because Lee was such a great actor and a fantastic Dracula figure. The 1977 BBC mini series *Dracula* starring Louis Jourdan, since it is a very true adaptation to the novel. The 1992 *Bram Stoker's Dracula* by Francis Ford Coppola; I loved Gary Oldman's portrayal of the Count.

**Does carrying the legacy of the Stoker name ever get burdensome?**
I would not say burdensome, I hold myself to a high standard regardless of my surname. Being a relative of Bram Stoker does open doors in the literary and film world, with that comes a responsibility to uphold our families reputation.

**What do you think Bram would make of the massive industry that has sprung up around his original story?**
I believe that Bram would have been very proud of the massive number of works which have been inspired by and adapted from his most famous

novel Dracula in many different forms. You must remember that Bram was a theatrical manager in addition to being a writer, he spent twenty-seven years adapting plays with his boss Sir Henry Irving to be staged at the Lyceum Theatre. To have a novel continue to be relevant for over a century on stage, in film and adapted into countless other forms of visual media, in literature, is certainly something that would have given Bram a lot of satisfaction.

# Epilogue

# The Last Sunrise

While writing this book I happened to listen to a podcast in which the illusionist Derren Brown was being asked about his thoughts on death. His response fascinated me. 'Nothing has meaning unless it's finite, right? If we lived forever ... we might like the idea for a second but actually, everything would very quickly become utterly meaningless and boring beyond measure.'

The obvious logic when discussing society's endless fascination with vampires is the immortality aspect, and that is certainly the attraction for most. But perhaps it is attractive because it is safely unreal – it's safe to imagine how marvellous it would be to exist as a glamorous, undead Creature Of The Night precisely because it is never going to happen.

Would you really want to be trapped with your own thoughts and feelings for eternity, while everyone around you either died at the end of a natural human lifespan or became undead monsters themselves, trapping you with *their* thoughts and feelings forever more? However much beauty and wealth one managed to accrue, the bottom line would be that you are stuck. Here. Forever. Perhaps it's not the eternal life we crave, but the eternal youth. Western society in particular often seems to value physical strength and beauty over almost everything else. Personality and intelligence is all for naught, the media tells us, if we're not also aesthetically attractive. Ageing dulls the glossy-skinned attributes of youth whether we like it or not and regardless of how many different skin creams we're fooled into buying. Made to feel as though the security of our place in the world is slipping, we are sucked too easily into the constant and ongoing battle against getting older – or, at least, not looking as thought the ageing process is affecting us.

We pump our financial worth into the billion dollar beauty business, whether through buying cosmetics to disguise our wrinkles and fading skin, or endless clothes that help us feel as though we're clinging on at least to life, if not exactly youth. Female actors are relegated to playing mothers and dotty aunts from the age of approximately 30 and while men seem to get a better deal with outside acceptance of the ageing process, they are certainly made to feel as though their value rests on their physical strength, virility and how much hair they've got left. It's no surprise, then, that the idea of never physically decaying is so tempting. The 'modern' vampire – those popular portrayals in book and on film since Polidori wrote *The Vampyre* in 1819 – is the epitome of immortal glamour. Whatever the era or geographical location in which a vampire story is set, we have come to expect certain basic standards.

Female vamps will invariably be thin and beautiful – to an almost ethereal level – but with a hidden darkness. After Lucy Westenra was turned in *Dracula*, she appeared as a wandering innocent in white flowing robes, her sharp teeth hidden behind rosebud lips. Lucy was a walking illustration of the dictionary definition of 'temptation' – until it was revealed that behind that coquettish smile was a heartless baby killer. Carmilla was a sweet young girl who just happened to lust after her female companions without having any compunctions about later draining them of life. If she doesn't look deceivingly innocent, then a female vamp will almost certainly be portrayed as a femme fatale, her dark eyes and crimson lips tempting unwary men to their doom.

Male vampires are invariably classically handsome. Christopher Lee might have made a terrifying Dracula, but he was attractive enough that his victims didn't ever seem to mind *too* much that his lordly lust was killing them. The Count who presents himself to Mina Murray in *Bram Stoker's Dracula* is a perfect gentleman in both appearance and manner. Sookie Stackhouse's love interests in *True Blood* are physically different, but each very attractive in their own way. Bill Compton is as dark as Eric is blond and between them they offer an all you can eat smörgåsbord of deadly sexuality. The enduring image of the vampire is one of the most glamorously romantic of all anti-heroes. But at the same time, we conveniently forget that the majority of vampire myths have their roots in those things that are designed to keep us in our place. The fear of death is one of the few things that could be said to frighten most people – even if we're not scared of the physical process of death, we probably have issues around being forced to leave this world before we're ready, before we've finished everything we want to do. Add to that the metaphysical fears that are installed in those who follow any religion in which the afterlife holds the threat of punishment for our perceived wrongs. Given that these wrongdoings are often seemingly arbitrary and put in place by the upholders of such religions, it can be a difficult business avoiding falling foul of them.

Vampire myths began during periods of fear and religious oppression, when to step away from the crowd could mean a social death, if not a literal one. If you were told that the disease that was decimating your family had been caused by a deceased relative rising from the grave, then you would probably do as you were told and go desecrate that corpse, because what are your other options? You either follow orders or risk being seen as part of the problem yourself. Those who 'don't belong' have been at risk ever since humankind lived in caves and relied on each other for security. Even in later eras when it has been physically possible to stay safe alone, that instinct is embedded into us – we *want* to belong.

Perhaps the real reason so many of us fall deeply in love with vampires is the fact that they are the same as us in many ways – they're just *better*. Sharper witted, better dressed and, above all, more confident. In the manner of a shark getting ready for another day of chomping on whatever gets in their way, vampires don't worry about what anyone else thinks of them. No middle-of-the-night angst for our bloodsucking heroes, they just Are. And isn't that what so many of us are searching for? The rock solid confidence that we in ourselves are 'enough' and anyone who disagrees should get out of our space or risk being eaten alive.

More than two centuries on from Polidori's Vampyre and nearly 125 years after Bram Stoker first published Dracula, it is clear that our desire for the sharpest of fangs will never die. There is safety in the knowledge that bloodied immortality will never be more than a delicious fantasy.

'The meaning of life is that it stops.'
Franz Kafka

# A Short Chronology of Vampire History

**Vampires in various guises are mentioned throughout history – this chronology focuses purely on events mentioned within this book.**

**c.1181–92:** Walter Map writes *De Nugis Curialium*, or *Courtiers' Trifles*, in which he talks of revenants rising from the grave in order to wreak revenge on those who had done them wrong in life.

**Late 1100s:** William of Newburgh writes *Historia Rerum Anglicarum* (*History of the Affairs of the English*)

**c.1300:** *Sefer Hasidim*, or *Book of the Pious*, includes a story about Astryiah, who sucks victims' blood with her hair.

**c.1428/31–1476/77:** lifespan of Vlad Țepeș (Vlad III Dracula, voivode of Wallachia).

**1597:** King James VI/I publishes *Daemonologie, In Forme of a Dialogue,* within which he muses on the ways in which incubi might impregnate human women.

**1614:** Countess Elizabeth Báthory de Ecsed dies while under house arrest, having been accused of the torture and murder of young women in her employ.

**1726:** Arnold Paole dies of a broken neck in Serbia; subsequent sickness among his fellow villagers was blamed on Paole having become a vampire.

**1731:** Johann Flückinger investigates supposed vampire attacks in a Serbian village. His report is mentioned in *The London Journal* in 1732, becoming the first known reference to vampires in the English press.

**1746:** Augustin Calmet publishes *Dissertations sur les apparitions des anges, des demons et des esprits, et sure les revenants et vampires de Hongrie, de Bohme.*

**1748:** Publication of *The Vampire*, a short poem by Heinrich Ossenfelder.

**1764:** Horace Walpole publishes *The Castle of Otranto*, widely accepted to be the first 'Gothic' novel.

**1764:** Voltaire's *Dictionnaire Philosophique* includes an entry for vampires.

**1810:** John Stagg publishes *The Vampyre* as part of his poetry collection, *Minstrel of the North*.

**1813:** Publication of *The Giaour,* a poem by Lord Byron.

**1819:** Publication of *The Vampyre*, book by John William Polidori.

**1845:** The first instalment of *Varney the Vampire* by James Malcolm Rymer is published as a 'penny dreadful' pamphlet.

**1866:** Ann 'Nan' Train is murdered by her cousin, John Moss, in Old Swan, Liverpool

**1872:** publication of *Carmilla*, a novella by Sheridan Le Fanu.

**1878:** John Payne writes *Lautrec*, a poem about a female vampire.

**1892:** Lena 'Mercy' Brown dies in Rhode Island – her heart and lungs are cut out and burned in the belief that she was a vampire

**1897:** Publication of *Dracula*, a Gothic horror novel by Bram Stoker.

**1914:** Fox Studios release *The Stain*, with Theda Bara (credited under her birth name of Theodora Goodman) as 'The Vampire'.

**1922:** Release of the silent movie *Nosferatu: eine Symphonie des Grauens*, directed by F.W. Murnau.

**1931:** *Dracula*, starring Bela Lugosi, is released and becomes the first sound film adaptation of Stoker's novel.

**1954:** The 'Gorbals Vampire Incident' occurs in Glasgow when large numbers of children gather in the city's Necropolis after reports of a vampire killing local children.

**1955:** The Children and Young Persons (Harmful Publications) Act passes into law, banning 'horror comics'. The Act was brought in almost entirely due to the activity in the Gorbals the previous year.

**1958:** Hammer Films release *Dracula,* starring Christopher Lee as the titular Count.

**1964–66:** *The Munsters* runs for seventy episodes across two seasons on CBS in the US.

**1966–71:** *Dark Shadows* appears on the ABC network in the USA; it hits its peak of popularity with the arrival of vampire character Barnabas Collins, ten months into its run.

**1967:** Release of *The Fearless Vampire Killers*, comedy horror film written and directed by Roman Polanski.

**1970:** *Vampire Lovers* is released, directed by Roy Ward and starring Ingrid Pitt.

**1970:** David Farrant claims to have witnessed a 'supernatural being' roaming the western section of Highgate Cemetery, north London.

**1970:** Sean Manchester declares Farrant's sighting to have been of an 'Eastern European vampire' and declares his intent to exorcise it from the graveyard.

**1972:** Hammer Film Productions release *Dracula A.D. 1972*, starring Peter Cushing and Christopher Lee.

**1972:** Count von Count makes his debut appearance on *Sesame Street*.

**1973:** *Blade* makes his first appearance in a Marvel comic.

**1976:** Publication of *Interview with a Vampire*, the first of Ann Rice's *The Vampire Chronicles* series of novels.

**1979:** Film release of *Love At First Bite*, starring George Hamilton.

**1979:** English post-punk band Bauhaus release *Bela Lugosi's Dead*, widely credited with being the first 'gothic rock' single.

**1981:** *The Hunger* by Whitley Strieber is published.

**1983:** *The Hunger* is adapted for cinematic release, starring Catherine Deneauve and David Bowie.

**1983:** A young mother reports fears of vampiric activity in the Toxteth area of Liverpool.

**1987:** *The Lost Boys* is released, directed by Joel Schumacher.

**1992:** Joss Whedan's original film version of *Buffy the Vampire Slayer* is released, starring Kristie Swanson as Buffy.

**1992:** Francis Ford Coppola's *Bram Stoker's Dracula* is released, widely considered to be the adaptation that stays closest to the original text.

**1992:** Publication of *Lost Souls* by Poppy Z. Brite.

**1993:** Publication of *Guilty Pleasures*, first in the 'Anita Blake, Vampire Hunter' series of novels by Laurell K. Hamilton.

**1994:** Neil Jordan's film adaptation of *Interview with the Vampire* is released.

**1995:** Release of *Dracula: Dead and Loving It*, starring Leslie Neilsen.

**1996:** Cinema release of *From Dusk Till Dawn*, written by and starring Quentin Tarantino, alongside George Clooney.

**1997–2003:** *Buffy the Vampire Slayer* runs on television, starring Sarah Michelle Gellar in the title role.

**1997:** Musical *Tanz Der Vampire* premieres in Austria and continued touring until the Covid-19 pandemic closed theatres worldwide in early 2020.

**2000:** Otto von Chriek makes his debut in *The Truth*, the twenty-fifth novel in Terry Pratchett's *Discworld* series.

**2001:** The first of Charlaine Harris's Sookie Stackhouse books, *Dead Until Dark*, is released. *The Southern Vampire Mysteries* would continue to be published at a rate of one book per year until 2013.

**2004:** Publication of *Let The Right One In*, book by John Ajvide Lindqvist.

**2004:** Publication of *Undead and Unwed*, the first in a series of novels by MaryJanice Davidson about modern-day vampire, Elizabeth 'Betsy' Taylor.

**2005:** Publication of *Twilight*, by Stephanie Meyer. Followed by *New Moon* (2006), *Eclipse* (2007), Breaking Dawn (2008).

**2006:** Elton John and Bernie Taupin's musical *Lestat* opens on Broadway to resoundingly negative reviews and runs for a mere nine weeks.

**2008:** Film adaptation of *Let The Right One In* is released, directed by Tomas Alfredson.

**2008:** Release of the film adaptation of *Twilight*, the first of five movies making up *The Twilight Saga*. Followed by *New Moon* (2009), *Eclipse* (2010), *Breaking Dawn – Part 1* (2011), *Breaking Dawn – Part 2* (2012).

**2008:** *True Blood*, the television adaptation of Charlaine Harris's *Southern Vampire Mysteries* books, is first broadcast by HBO – it would go on to run for seven seasons until 2014.

**2008:** The pilot episode of *Being Human* appears on BBC Three in the UK. Following several cast changes, the show ran for five series on the same channel, between 2009–2013.

**2010:** Publication of *The Radleys* by Matt Haig.

**2012:** Release of *Byzantium*, directed by Neil Jordan and starring Gemma Arterton and Saoirse Ronan.

**2013:** Cinema release of *Only Lovers Left Alive*, starring Tilda Swinton and Tom Hiddleston.

**2014:** Film release of *What We Do In The Shadows*, horror-comedy 'mockumentary' written and directed by Jemaine Clement and Taika Waititi, produced and set in New Zealand.

**2020:** Steven Moffatt and Mark Gatiss's television adaptation of *Dracula* is released through the BBC and Netflix, starring Claes Bang and Dolly Wells.

**2020:** Publication of *Midnight Sun*, the fifth book in the *Twilight* series by Stephanie Meyer.

**2021:** Britannia Pictures are due to release the first ever movie adaptation of Polidori's *The Vampyre*, directed by Rowan M. Ashe. Originally slated for release in 2019, at the time of writing this film is still listed only as being 'in development'.

# Bibliography

**Listings are for the books I have personally read and/or referenced. Older or newer versions (sometimes by other publishers) may be available.**

Aaronovitch, Ben, *Moon Over Soho*, Gollanz, 2011

Aaronovitch, Ben, *Rivers of London*, Gollanz, 2011

Brite, Poppy Z., *Lost Souls*, Penguin, 1994

Byron, Lord George Gordon. *The Giaour*, 1813 (public domain)

Caliban, Louisianax Elini Miriam, Ravensfield, Louis Paul (eds); Gutteridge, Duncan (illus.) *In Blood We Lust*, Dark Angel Press, 1999

Calmet, Antoine Augustin, *The Phantom World: the History and Philosophy of Spirits, Apparitions, &c*, 1746, (public domain)

Cohen, David, *The Psychology of Vampires*, Routledge, 2019

Davidson, MaryJanice, *Undead and Unwed*, Piatkus Books, 2006

Glasfurd, Guinevere, *The Year Without Summer*, Two Roads, 2020

Haig, Matt, *The Radleys*, Canongate Books, 2010

Hamilton, Laurell K., *Guilty Pleasures*, Orbit, 1993

Harkness, Deborah, *A Discovery of Witches*, Penguin Books, 2011

Harkness, Deborah, *Shadow of Night*, Penguin Books, 2012

Harris, Charlaine, *Dead Until Dark*, Ace Books, 2001

Hoffs, Gill, *The Sinking of the RMS Tayleur*, Pen & Sword, 2014

King James VI of Scotland, *Daemonologie, In Forme of a Dialogue, Divided into three Books: By the High and Mighty Prince, James &c*, 1597 (public domain)

Le Fanu, Sheridan, *Carmilla*, 1872 (public domain)

Lindqvist, John Ajvide, *Let The Right One In*, Quercus, 2007

Mackenzie, Donald Alexander, *Scottish Folklore and Folk Life – Studies in Race, Culture and Tradition*, Blackie & Son Limited, 1935

Map, Walter, *De Nugis Curialium*, foreword by M.R. James, University Press, Oxford, 1983

Meyer, Stephenie, *Twilight*, Little, Brown and Co., 2005
Ossenfelder, Heinrich, *Der Vampire*, 1748, (public domain)
Poe, Edgar Allan, *The Premature Burial*, 1844, (public domain)
Polidori, John William, *The Vampyre*, Woodstock Books, 2001
Pratchett, Terry, *Carpe Jugulum*, Doubleday, 1998
Pratchett, Terry, *The Fifth Elephant*, Doubleday, 1999
Pratchett, Terry, *The Truth*, Doubleday, 2000
Pratchett, Terry, *Monstrous Regiment*, Doubleday, 2003
Pratchett, Terry, *Unseen Academicals*, Doubleday, 2009
Reece, Dr Gregory L., *Creatures of the Night*, I.B.Tauris, 2012
Rice, Anne, *Interview with the Vampire*, Knopf, 1976
Rice, Anne, *Queen of the Damned*, Sphere, 2008
Shelley, Mary, *Frankenstein; or, The Modern Prometheus*, 1818 (public domain)
Stoker, Bram, *Dracula*, 1897 (public domain)
Strieber, Whitley, *The Hunger*, Simon and Schuster, 2008
Voltaire, aka François Marie Arouet, *Dictionnaire Philosophique*, 1764, (public domain)
Walpole, Horace, *The Castle of Otranto*, 1764 (public domain)
Whitman, Walt, *Leaves of Grass*, 1855 (public domain)

# Filmography

*A Fool There Was*. Dir. Frank Powell, Fox Studios, 1915

*Blade*. Dir. Stephen Norrington, New Line Cinema, 1998

*Bram Stoker's Dracula*. Dir. Francis Ford Coppola, Columbia Pictures, 1992

*Buffy the Vampire Slayer*. Dir. Franz Rubel Kuzui, 20th Century Fox, 1992

*Byzantium*. Dir. Neil Jordan, StudioCanal (UK), IFC Films (US), 2012

*Dracula* (released as *Horror of Dracula* in the US). Dir. Terence Fisher, Rank Film (UK), Universal-International (International), 1958

*Dracula A.D. 1972*. Dir. Alan Gibson, Columbia-Warner (UK), Warner Bros. (US), 1972

*Dracula: Dead and Loving It*. Dir. Mel Brooks, Sony Pictures Releasing, 1995

*From Dusk Till Dawn*. Dir. Robert Rodriguez, Dimension Films, 1996

*Interview With The Vampire*. Dir. Neil Jordan, Warner Bros., 1994

*Love At First Bite*. Dir. Stan Dragoti, American International Pictures, 1979

*Nosferatu: eine Symphonie des Grauens (Nosferatu: a Symphony of Horror)*. Dir. F.W. Murnau, Prana-Film, 1922

*Only Lovers Left Alive*. Dir. Jim Jarmusch, Pandora Film Verleih (Germany) 2013, Soda Pictures (UK) 2014

*Razor Blade Smile*. Dir. Jake West, Manga Entertainment, 1998

*Shadow of the Vampire*. Dir. E. Elias Merhige, Lions Gate Films, 2000

*The Fearless Vampire Killers*. Dir. Roman Polanski, Metro-Goldwyn-Mayer, 1967

*The Hunger*. Dir. Tony Scott, MGM/UA Entertainment Co., 1983

*The Lost Boys*. Dir. Joel Schumacher, Warner Bros., 1987

*The Twilight Saga: Breaking Dawn – Part 1*. Dir. Bill Condon, Summit Entertainment, 2011

*The Twilight Saga: Breaking Dawn – Part 2*. Dir. Bill Condon, Summit Entertainment, 2012

*The Twilight Saga: Eclipse*. Dir. David Slade, Summit Entertainment, 2010

*The Twilight Saga: New Moon*. Dir. Chris Weitz, Summit Entertainment, 2009

*Twilight*. Dir. Catherine Hardwicke, Summit Entertainment, 2008

*What We Do In The Shadows*. Dir. Jemaine Clement, Taika Waititi; Madman Entertainment (New Zealand), Paramount Pictures, The Orchard (North America), 2014

# Index